American Dream Women

American Dream Women

Insuring Women's Wealth

Second Edition

Mary Lynn Seebeck

WestWind Press
North Richland Hills, Texas

WestWind Press
An imprint of D. & F. Scott Publishing, Inc.
P.O. Box 821653
N. Richland Hills, TX 76182
817 788-2280
info@dfscott.com
www.dfscott.com

Printed in the United States of America
09 08 07 06 05 5 4 3 2 1

Library of Congress Cataloging-in-Publication Data
Seebeck, Mary Lynn, 1939-
  American dream women : insuring women's wealth / Mary Lynn Seebeck.--
2nd ed.
    p. cm.
  Includes bibliographical references and index.
  ISBN 1-930566-52-2 (hard cover : alk. paper)
  1. Women--Finance, Personal. 2. Investments. I. Title.
  HG179.S382 2005
  332.024'0082--dc22

                        2005008793

AXA Financial Compliance Control Number: **AGE-81677 (11/12)(exp. 11/14)**

Cover Design by Suzette Johnson
Portrait Photography of Mary Lynn Seebeck by Gittings, Dallas

Each woman measures wealth differently. Women have defined "being" wealthy as being: comfortable, well paid, financially independent, able to laugh all the way to the bank, able to spend without worry, able to have security for a rainy day, and able to run a profitable business. Tangibles associated with wealth include: a nest egg, financial resources, investment accounts, stocks and bonds, assets, property, and riches.

The women who have inspired this book have further defined their own wealth, not in any dollar amount, but as a future condition that improves life beyond what they experience today. Ideas women have shared include: knowing my freezer will always be full and my pantry will be diversified with essentials and goodies; outfitting children with more than one pair of shoes, clothing that fits them as they grow, and a wardrobe for each season; taking family vacations at will; being able to give children dance and music lessons; having no loans or credit card debt; living in a home that's paid for; paying for college without loans; living off an inheritance; maintaining my current lifestyle when I retire; being able to comfortably pay myself as well as my employees and to offer them excellent benefits; and leaving a legacy for children or a charitable institution.

Wealth encompasses a spirit and state of "being" as much as it refers to a condition of "having." This book is for all women striving and accomplishing wealth—on their own terms.

Important Caution to the Reader

This book does not take the place of a personal review and financial needs analysis as performed by qualified professionals for the purpose of determining financial, legal, or tax advice for a personal or business financial program. You are encouraged to seek advice from financial professionals who are licensed, experienced, and/or certified.

The contents of this book represent the views of the author. Therefore, the information contained herein does not necessarily reflect the opinions of any insurance or financial services company. This book is for informational purposes only and is based on a general understanding of the subject matter discussed. You should discuss your personal situation with your tas, legal, or professional advisors efore implementing any strategy..

For instructional purposes throughout, the examples use compound interest tables, and average an assumed 5 percent annual rate of return over the time period. Due to market fluctuation, past performance is not a guarantee of future results, and there is no guarantee of future results.

"A Circle of Women"

Seen here are some of the many women and their families who have inspired this book. They demonstrate that disciplined planning is helping them gain control of their financial future.

Contents

PREFACE
A Philosophy Based on Teaching

Throughout the course of life, women give their time and talents to make the world a better place—for loved ones, for communities, and for humanity. Entering the third millennium, American women enjoy educational, economic, political, and social opportunities that are unequaled anywhere in the world. Such privilege is increasing women's capacity to give back to their families and communities—not only through humanitarian pursuits, but financially as well.

I have watched my own daughters and women clients climb to levels of educational and career achievement that I never thought possible when I was growing up in the post-WW II era. Some women are earning incomes at wonderful and staggering rates. But many women have made financial mistakes and have readjusted their strategies to gradually reach their goals. Women are now a majority in America by several million. With more women working and earning higher incomes than ever before, women's keen awareness of financial planning is imperative in order to accumulate wealth from such unprecedented income earning potential. The economic, insurance, investment, and banking conditions that create this financial environment in the United States offer unique and unparalleled opportunities for us to accumulate wealth for ourselves and the children, parents, businesses, and employees who depend on us. To achieve the wealth that can come from disciplined savings and sound planning, we must attain knowledge, demonstrate creativity, exhibit courage, and assume accountability for determining our own financial futures.

For more than thirty-five years I've been involved in sales and marketing, both with my father's family business and my own insurance and financial services practice. Over the course of this career, most of my women customers and clients have shared their life experiences with me in the expectation that others may learn from their successes and failures. It is this spirit that has driven the creation of this book.

Twelve Steps For Success

Part 1 provides twelve steps to help gain control of your financial future. The individual chapters focus on creating a comfort level and sense of urgency to take command of your personal finances and teaching you a step-by-step process by which to do so. The need for working with a professional team that will stay with you and assist you in monitoring your progress as your life needs change is explained and emphasized.

The twelve steps are:

- coordinating a team of advisors
- selecting them
- interviewing to find the right match for your personal style
- learning how to identify unethical behavior
- knowing what you want
- assessing your present financial health
- determining what you can afford
- understanding your company benefits
- coordinating company and personal planning
- learning how to diversify savings, insurance, and investments for now and the future
- controlling the buying process
- selecting a company, products and progress updates

After reading the first part, you should have an insider's view of fundamentals of insurance and financial strategies.

Part 2 features the needs that are most prevalent among my clients and offers planning strategies to help solve those needs. The family profiles, which are the core of this section, are nonfictional accounts given by some of the thousand women and men who are served by my practice. Their stories tell about their lives alone, with a partner, with children, with businesses, and with parents. Names have been changed, but the experiences have not. The stories of women's lives address the circumstances and needs appealing to single women, recent college graduates beginning professional careers, women taking care of aging parents or special needs children, single parent moms, dual-income families, wives managing a wealthy husband's money, professionals, women business owners, widows, and self-made women wealthy in their own right.

Throughout my practice, I've served hundreds of women who have expressed common needs, wants, and desires for the future. The personal stories they share in part 2 are organized according to life cycles. If you are like most members of our focus group, you will scan the table of contents to find the story that fits your current lifestyle and circumstances and go back to read the others as your life changes. Each story is independent and complete on its own and provides background, questions to ask, needs, and possible solutions.

The objective of this book is not to teach you about technical products. The objective is to teach you how to attain knowledge; to ask the right questions of professionals; to paint a larger picture of the many facets of accounting, legal provisions, insurance, and investments and how they must work together if you ultimately want to gain financial independence and achieve your financial goals.

This book is about the heart and core of how you can financially protect yourself and those you love—throughout your life, with or without a partner. It is not a technical treatise about the complex world of specific insurance or investment products. Licensed professionals are competent to teach you about these concepts or products on a face-to-face basis. I do emphasize, however, that all women seeking financial guidance must be knowledgeable enough to ask the right questions, demand to be taught, and ensure that the members of their professional team are licensed, experienced, and/ or credentialed.

When financial professionals and certified public accountants (CPAs) approach these stories, they will see that the financial strategies proposed throughout are cross functional and interdisciplinary. Strategies use mutual funds, investments, an-

nuities, certificates of deposit, and life insurance products, together with various legal provisions where appropriate, to satisfy
short- and long-term goals.

A Philosophy Based on Teaching

This book is based on the central psychological premise that the
process used by most women to make decisions about their future
is markedly different than the process employed by most men. My
philosophy for working with clients advocates a relationship
approach rather than a transaction approach. This relationship
approach forms the foundation of my business practice—as well
as of this book. The relationship approach poses a fundamental
belief that women prefer to make decisions about their financial
futures based on developing long-term relationships that can
teach them and help them develop confidence over time.

As such, the approach I pose in this book precludes a transaction or product-oriented sale based on a one-time interaction or purchase that does not consider the total picture of a woman's financial
situation (her current income and expenses relative to her dreams,
wants, needs, and desires for the future). My philosophy advocates
that members of a woman's professional financial team provide her
ongoing communication and knowledge through a teaching process.
In fact, I am adamant that financial strategies for women that are
based on transaction selling rather than relationship selling are
inappropriate for most women because their methodology is generally contrary to women's decision-making processes.

A Process for Continuous Improvement

Business or professional women active in corporate or private firms
may recognize the thread of Total Quality Management (TQM)
weaving a tapestry throughout this essay. Using a TQM approach
offers a process by which personal planning can be adopted with
ease until it becomes habit. A personal mission or goal is identified
in terms of women's long-term desires. Assessment relative to
selecting financial guidance, earning cycles, and saving cycles
plays a major part in the process. Planning a financial program is

followed by a disciplined commitment to implement the plan. Annual reviewing and adjusting the plan for incremental progress are a must if a program is to succeed in its mission of financial independence or accumulating wealth over time. The secret to accumulating wealth is to make the process dynamic, focused, and ongoing so that it becomes habitual. For some women, this means a major shift in the way they have been conditioned to think as opposed to the way they *must* think and act if they are to prosper financially. The TQM model of defining goals, doing an annual assessment, planning, implementing, and reviewing provides a track to run on that will adjust with personal circumstances through all cycles of life. It is a process that advocates an active relationship between a woman and all members on her team of professionals.

Neither a twelve-step process nor the personal financial strategy a woman creates can succeed without her commitment and discipline. A woman who expresses herself through athletics, music, art, dance, writing, or other style of performance acknowledges the need for continuous development and determination if she is to succeed. If she has a dream, vision, or goal, she also needs the talent, skill, and discipline to carry it out. She cannot rely on someone else to perform for her. Life will bring chaotic days, high-energy days, and low-energy days. All affect her ability to carry out her mission and vision and achieve her dream. But if she is focused on her dream, ultimately her athletic achievement, her performances, her paintings, her songs, her poems, or her sculptures are born and accumulate over time to build a collection that celebrates her discipline of achievement. I believe this discipline, if applied as a mindset and lifestyle can likewise yield financial wealth accumulation over time for American women disciplined enough to remain focused on the beauty and joy of their vision.

It is my hope that this book will provide a step-by-step winning process as well as confidence and encouragement to any woman who strives to control and balance her financial power. May you achieve confidence and the self-determination to secure the future wealth that can provide for you and those who depend on you in the twenty-first century.

Mary Lynn Seebeck

Ft. Worth, Texas

DEDICATION

—— *Susie* ——

Holy Angels was an all-girl Catholic academy in Milwaukee, Wisconsin. I met Susie there as we entered our freshman year of high school in 1953. She was from a family of ten children; I from a family of five. We shared similar responsibilities for family chores and taking care of our younger brothers and sisters. But it was the Friday night dances, dates, and boys that sparked the bond that linked us in these tender years and ultimately—for life.

In high school, we were together all day. These were the times for poodle skirts, pony tails and saddle shoes, chatting, planning, dreaming and knowing every secret there was to know about each other—while a tiny transistor radio beat the Rock 'n Roll of the 1950s.

Susie was the quiet one, and I was the spunky, spirited redhead most likely to get into trouble. At sixteen, we were driving around in my 1956 powder blue Ford convertible with a Thunderbird engine. We earned much attention from the boys back then!

After graduation, we proceeded to work in our family businesses. Susie was her father's clerical assistant in their dry cleaning business. My father's business consisted of five gas stations, and he made me do a little of everything including accounts receivable, administering fuel oil sales, and, of course, pumping gas. Susie and I believed our Dads loved us enough to keep us busy so that we had no time to get into trouble. We both eventually married our high school sweethearts.

Susie was married ten years before adopting a son, Eric. Soon after, Christopher arrived and then Bradley. With a phone call or visit, we daily shared our happy times as we raised our families.

After nineteen years, Susie's marriage ended in divorce. She faced the responsibilities of raising Eric, Christopher, and Bradley, who were ages thirteen, ten, and seven, respectively. She was over-whelmed, frightened, angry, and stressed with worry as she juggled work, children, and finances as a single mom. This was not the hap-pily-ever-after story we had dreamed about as young teens.

We spent much time together then, playing games with the children, taking them to the park for picnics, and taking time as friends to lean on each other. It was tough to see my best friend giv-ing so much of herself without direction or knowing where her life was going. I felt helpless to make a difference.

After six years as a single mom, Susie fell in love and mar-ried John in 1984. The three boys were in tuxedos at a quaint cer-emony in a small country church; I was her attendant. The reception at a golf course, where she and John had courted, painted a lovely picture of a new secure future for her, and the expectation of many years of happiness.

Soon after her remarriage, my husband, Tom, and I moved to Texas to follow Tom's career. I signed a career contract as an agent and began my journey into the insurance business. Susie was my greatest supporter as we exchanged weekly updates about our lives. On numerous occasions she asked me to create an insurance pro-gram for her and explained that if anything ever happened to her, she did not want John to have the financial responsibility of raising the boys. Because she was my best friend, I felt that I needed to know absolutely everything about every product and the intricacies of insurance before I felt adequate to satisfy her request.

Ten months after I began selling life insurance, we were talk-ing during one of our weekly updates on the phone; we discussed her concerns and determined that Susie needed $1,500 income each month in the event that she became disabled and $250,000 of life insurance protection to provide for her sons. I was planning a trip to Wisconsin the following May, and we would complete the paperwork at that time.

In April, a month before my scheduled trip, the call came. It was Susie telling me something a best friend never wants to hear. She was hospitalized with lung cancer. I was devastated; of course this news did not make sense since I was at that time a chain smoker.

Susie was hopeful for a full recovery, and, knowing how important a patient's state of mind is, John and I joined the doctors in providing hope and encouragement.

I was overwhelmed and angry at myself for not having the self-confidence necessary to help her when she had originally asked for help. I had spent a year calling on businesses and strangers while letting my best friend go uncovered. I felt no sense of urgency, because I thought I would have her forever.

For the next eighteen months, I shuttled back and forth from Texas to Wisconsin to be with Susie. We made visits to her doctor to hear his encouraging words. Praying that she would get better, I envisioned the possibility of her passing several years cancer free. If she was then in remission, hopefully she would be considered insurable, and I could fulfill the commitment that I was not confident enough to handle earlier.

During one visit on a clear and beautiful day, we drank tea in her back yard under the pines. We were alone and happy to have quiet time. She told me how happy she was with John and how good he was to her and to the boys. She also relayed the fears that she had of not being able to fight the cancer and that she was not yet ready to leave this world.

Susie was concerned about not being able to enjoy her sons' college days, their marriages, and the children she hoped they would have. We hugged and cried, fearful of the future. Neither one of us mentioned the insurance program that never came to fruition, but I knew Susie was disheartened. I was overwhelmed and without words; nothing I could say could ever fix my lack of responsiveness to her request.

Back in Texas, I prayed for Susie to be well again, for her family, and for the day she would again be insurable. I watched my dear friend struggle against cancer, emotionally giving her boys and John everything she had. However, the bitter truth was that during her disability, her income was not there to assist the family—because I had not taken care of her need when she was healthy. I had not been confident or ready enough to sell insurance to my best friend. In 1986, eighteen months after being diagnosed with lung cancer, Susie was back in the hospital. After the call, I closed my office in Texas and flew to Wisconsin to be with her.

At the hospital, John asked me to break the news to Susie. Two and a half years after I entered the insurance business, I was faced with telling my best friend that she was dying. At 7:30 am, I closed the door to face her in her hospital room. This friend of mine, who had shared so many dreams with me, soon would not be around to share more. We looked at each other, and I said, "Susie, you are dying; I'm here." She nodded; she already knew it in her heart.

She thanked me for being with her and continued by adding that I was a great friend and that she was thankful for the memories. As her frail body lay in the hospital bed, she looked at me and said, "Mary, I've been fighting death because my affairs are not in order. I am running out of time, and I need your help. I want John to receive the little I have. Since you are my financial professional and best friend, I know you will know how to do this." We set about getting Susie's financial affairs in order by appointing her husband, John, as beneficiary of the policy. I arranged for her to spend her last days in a hospice, so the boys and John could enjoy her time uninterrupted.

I wrote down her wishes about her assets and arranged for all to be notarized. Then, my dying friend said to me, "Mary, don't ever be ashamed of what you do. You have so much to give and so many people to talk to, for I have learned that insurance is the greatest gift anyone could give. I have forgiven you and myself, for failing to have my financial affairs in order." This is when I was able to tell Susie how sorry I was for not putting her insurance in place when she first asked me.

Even though she forgave me, it didn't change her family's financial position. I was feeling incredible guilt and never wanted to make the same mistake again. I never again wanted to say, "I'm sorry" for leaving a client unprotected. I was confused but knew that she would tell me the truth about what she would have done to protect her family if she could turn the clock back and do the planning all over again. We talked about insurance, disability protection, and investments. And I asked her what sequence and priority she felt each of these had when satisfying her dreams for her family.

With a confidence that came with thinking about it over and over all these months, she explained in her frail voice, "Protect income first, Mary. With disability protection, I could have given so much more to John and the boys. It broke my heart to see them sacrifice when I could no longer work. It could have helped John with the medical expenses. The $1,500 monthly disability check we talked about would have gone a long way." She continued, "Life insurance coverage is second, Mary. The $250,000 life insurance policy could have provided a college fund. Investments should be considered last. The modest amount I received from my divorce settlement earned hardly anything, and what little it did earn I used for the boys. Just think how much life insurance that sum could have purchased."

She was getting tired but smiled; I could see a new calm beginning to settle over her. I knew at that moment that Susie's gift to me was to resolve this for me for the future. As Susie described what was important, she said nothing about how well known the insurance company was, nothing about any specific products, nothing about term insurance versus whole life insurance, premiums or dividends— all concepts and phrases that agents get wrapped up in when they lose focus about the purpose of insurance. Susie explained that needs and feelings come first.

We held hands and continued to share our life's memories that morning. We cried and laughed, and I polished her nails for the last time. As we said our last Rosary together, she relaxed and found peace. Susie died soon after, at the age of forty-seven, leaving Eric, Christopher, Bradley, and her dear love, John.

As I cried in the airplane on my trip back to Texas, I wrote my commitment about how I would serve my clients from that day forward. I would listen to their needs and dreams, and review their income, expenses, and assets in relationship to their dreams, wants, needs, and desires. I would discuss disability income coverage first, life insurance second, and investments, third—only after the insurance was in place.

It is Susie who is my motivation to dedicate my life to this great industry and the legacy it provides for families. She is truly beside me every day, and I remain ever committed to first satisfy the needs of women everywhere—especially those of friends and those who are dearest to me.

PART I
12 Steps to Help Gain Control of Your Financial Future

Achieving the American Dream

America was built on a dream, and the dream continues. The vision of a promised land of opportunity where you can accomplish anything if you only work hard enough has been a driving force for generations of immigrant and American families.

In the last fifty years, demographic changes in the American family and the American workplace have rewritten the rules of the American dream. The number of women in the civilian labor force working outside the home has increased dramatically and single and married working women with responsibilities for children has substantially increased. It is estimated that there are millions of single parents. More than ever, American women are facing responsibilities to pursue and achieve the American dream—alone and as heads of households, families, and businesses.

The escalation of American women attaining undergraduate and postgraduate degrees has likewise created a new drive for American women to pursue higher paying jobs and to gain financial independence. Independence is a catalyst for self-actualization. The increase of women earning educational degrees has grown to heights unmatched anywhere in the world.

However, women cannot rely on their success in academics or business to achieve success in the financial world. The successful behaviors that women have learned in their journey through academic life do not necessarily prepare us for what is necessary to accumulate financial wealth on our own. Studying hard, working hard, and giving a job or career 150 percent do not accumulate financial wealth.

I was born and raised in the Ozzie and Harriet generation when expectations were well-defined regarding my role as a wife and mother. My life then was not much different than that of many American women my age. I was responsible for making the house a home and taking care of the children. When I eventually entered the working world and pursued professional education after raising my family, *all* of this was fit in after I had my home and family responsibilities satisfied. The basics of daily family life such as grocery shopping, planning meals, doing laundry, keeping a clean and orderly home, and raising children were priorities *before* my career. All competed for my time. After I started my own business, the multiple responsibilities intensified.

Because there are only twenty-four hours in a day, my husband also shared with the family responsibilities. In my generation, it was the husband's role in the family to take care of the business of car insurance, home insurance, and retirement, if any planning was done. For most families, assuring that the daily expenses and emergencies were covered was such a predominant concern that rarely could we even think about what we would need for retirement forty years into the future.

In the 1960s, when the women's movement and the necessity of a two-income earning household brought women into the workplace in large numbers, many women were satisfied to assign the primary responsibility for family security to the husband's income. Women were generally content with whatever medical insurance and term life insurance was provided for their husbands by the companies where they worked; the husband's coverage was primary. Women relied on the company where their husbands worked to know what was right for them and were comfortable with the thought that as long as the company plans were available, families were in some way "safe and secure."

Many educated, professional women working in corporate America or working in their own family businesses never dream that a day will come when their company benefits, dads, or husbands will not be there to help attend to these matters.

When the romance and beauty of marriage and raising young children become priorities for a woman, a loving, spirited and gentle-hearted woman does not think that someday her life could be very different. Someday she could be alone. When marriage is good, and life is going according to plan, a woman does not want to plan for the worst. To do so seems like an act of doom or an admission of little faith or trust.

Women generally believe in trust and goodness and light. Living in the worlds we create, we believe that we have dominion over our homes, our families, and our lives. We believe that our lives are stories and that we can write our own chapters. That is how women write their American Dream. As women, we believe that if we give all of our energy and love to make our marriages prosper and if we give all of our time to our jobs and career, we will surely reap great rewards. We want it to be so.

When a woman wills positive energy into her home or family, she usually carries the expectation of positive results. Therefore, most women do not believe that their positive efforts and energies can turn out wrong or take a turn for the worst. Most women do not believe that another woman could capture their husbands' attention. Most women do not believe that with their loyalty, creativity, flawless education, and prospective contributions to a company, the boss who hired them would stop believing in them one day. A woman usually does not believe that the company she gives her life to will let her go or outplace her, especially when she has put her career first and sacrificed a great deal in her family life to do so. When a woman is focused on climbing the ladder of success in corporate America, or medical institutions or academia, her focus is on doing her best job. Planning for the tables to turn in life is to accommodate negative thoughts that impair positive thinking.

This state of mind that many American women bring to life is a positive one. However, it does not prepare them to live or work in environments still dominated by patriarchal values and methods of learning. Women are often the last to learn that people don't have money or wealth by becoming educated and working hard. A college degree alone will not do it. Success can not do it. We must do it for ourselves. We can create wealth by implementing tactics and strategies for saving on a monthly basis.

Differing Values about Control

There is a great dichotomy between the values that women and men bring to living—values that affect the way they approach financial accumulation and values that affect the way buying decisions are made.

As young boys and growing adults, men are taught that life is war, not a fairy tale. Competition and winning are keys for survival. Creativity ensures supremacy. Life is a war to be won by tactics and strategies. That paradigm also defines how men create families and companies. It determines how men approach the accumulation of financial wealth. Someone is always there to challenge them; so they are forever ready with tactics and strategies in hand for winning. This is true whether they are being Boy Scouts, racing cars, playing sports, or building a corporate empire. Men generally believe that someone is always competing with them to sack the yardage they have gained—any jeopardy can happen, it must be controlled and protected with all options open, options and strategies with the boss, options and strategies with business associates, options and strategies with women, options and strategies with money. Men are taught that success comes from *being in control.*

For men, financial security is another priority on the chess board of life because they do not want to be held in check—caught unprotected. Their planning is a series of maneuvers through which they demonstrate an upper hand and by which they demonstrate superiority among their associates. Bits and pieces of information about the latest products and strategies are coveted as maneuvers for winning the war. Men revel at the game. Each maneuver or financial strategy is based on new and better intelligence or counterintelligence provided by the agent or broker du jour. Therefore, with each step, a man gains confidence that the next strategy is the winning move—the one that will do it all for him. Men whom I have counseled, *appear* to be comfortable in the world of financial vehicles and money matters. Some buy the stocks that are hot, the insurance where the premiums and company are the most competitive, mutual funds today, or bonds tomorrow.

By contrast, as I've seen with my clients, many women have been raised in families where they learn *how not to be in control* or *to abdicate control* to someone else regarding financial matters. Habits and behaviors for gaining control are something they must relearn after they leave home—sometimes the hard way. I firmly believe the greatest gift a parent can give a daughter is to teach her how to become financially responsible, knowledgeable, and accountable at an early age.

Many women's lives have vehicles—other than financial vehicles—as their priorities; they play taxi for car pools and soccer games. The successful professional women I've worked with do not revel in absorption of the latest and greatest technical data; they do not revel in playing the game. Their satisfaction comes from knowing that solutions are put in place to solve their emotional wants and needs for now and for the future.

When women decide to become involved in their own financial affairs, the process is markedly different than scouting for the latest financial hot tip of the week. Women want to learn as they go. They want an extended educational process that demands complete explanations. They want to see solutions without complexity. Emotions, feelings, and a process of sharing are what matter.

Emotional Versus Technical Advice

The roles and behaviors that men and women learn create differences in how they approach the planning process. Because the banking, insurance, and finance industries are dominated by men, there is a dichotomy between the way women buy insurance or other financial products and the way these products are sold to women. It took me a long time to understand why I was having difficulty explaining to men the philosophy underlying the way I conduct my practice.

In the insurance industry, a company provides field agents with financial materials that illustrate cash values, dividend accumulation, and computer enhancements. The support is technical. It is rare to find a questionnaire that addresses a woman's emotional desires, dreams, and short- and long-term needs for the future. The questionnaires provided by companies are designed to elicit immediate answers from the prospective buyer. I don't believe that there are too many women who feel comfortable baring the truth about their lives until they understand a reason for doing so.

I've conducted joint sales work with many excellent agents. Together we have come to the conclusion that there are distinct differences in the process that most men and most women use to make buying decisions for financial services products. Men are inclined to be technical. It's natural for them; they emphasize financial facts and bypass the world of emotion. Consider their process like this:

Need or Want Cash ➔ Review Data ➔
Make Decision Based on Price or Competitive Feature ➔
Trust Based on + or – Outcome of Financial Advice

A man develops trust with a financial professional based on the monetary outcome—win or lose.

We have found that a woman's process is more like this:

Emotional Expression of Qualitative Needs ➔
Sharing of Common Values ➔
Questions and Answers Based on Teaching and Learning ➔
Confidence, Comfort, and Mutual Respect ➔ Trust Grows ➔
Consideration of Products for Purchase

A woman's process begins with emotion, followed by sharing, teaching, learning, developing confidence and trust *before* any discussion of products occurs.

One client of mine, Carol, is forty years old and married with two children. She recalls how it was years ago when she and her husband were meeting with agents. "All these years I sat and watched my husband with agents discussing life insurance around our dinner table. They looked and nodded at each other like they both knew what they were talking about. They didn't involve me in the discussion, and the agent was happy to discuss these things only with my husband. My husband never asked any questions. Now, my husband has openly admitted to me that he really doesn't know anything about life insurance; he just knew we needed some. I just looked at him dumbfounded; I couldn't believe it. My husband handled the life insurance, auto insurance, and house insurance. I handled everything else in our lives. I never understood life insurance and found that the agents did not talk to me but talked with my husband instead. I always thought my husband understood everything by the way he acted. Now twenty-two years later and twenty-two years older, I realize he is terribly underinsured, and I never had any policy of my own."

Some financial professionals with whom I've worked have had difficulty asking women buyers simple questions like, "Tell me something about each of your children." "Do you see your marriage as being long term?" "Do you enjoy your career?" "Do you plan to change companies?" "Is the company you're working for growing or experiencing any downsizing or layoffs?" These questions get at the core of why women are making plans. These emotional questions and issues that I address easily, many agents find irrelevant to discuss. As a woman agent, I want to know and understand the emotional motivations that are driving my women clients toward their financial goals.

I believe that most women initially require an emotional framework for their decision making that is based on a discussion of their wants, needs, and desires rather than a technical framework about product information.

The first time I was with a colleague on a sales call with a woman business owner, he talked about *split dollar* and *reverse split dollar*, which are technical terms involving the ownership and beneficiary arrangements of a cash value policy! I sat there amazed! I thought I was at a football game watching new plays I hadn't heard before. My understanding and discussion of such business insurance concepts is by the benefits they provide, not the technical jargon. I have found that discussing planning concepts with technical jargon doesn't fit comfortably into the language of the people I serve. My primary clients are business professionals, physicians, lawyers, CPAs, entrepreneurs, and the wealthy. I find that they want to be talked to in a way that can enable them to learn and understand rather than in a way that makes them feel they lack knowledge.

The difference between the emotional and the technical approach often causes frustration for women who seek to buy insurance or financial products. The availability of seasoned women agents does not meet the demand of the women's market. Most likely, women financial professionals have not had any women as mentors. There are few women directing financial services companies. There are few women who are part of corporate technical teams. As a result, women buyers are being approached with technical information and marketing tactics that presuppose that women think like men. I believe that this approach is not appropriate, adequate, or satisfying for the vast majority of women buyers.

Many financial professionals servicing women have a tendency to be preoccupied with illustrations, computer presentations, specific products, and all things analytical and technical during the sales call. This frustrates many women. When women buy insurance or investments, they need to demand that the products and policies are presented to them in a way that teaches them how the product addresses their emotional dreams, wants, needs, and desires. I've found that most women also want plenty of time to tell their life stories, analyze their mistakes, and enjoy the successes they've made along the way. Focusing on technical support and data is not the way to begin developing a relationship that will last for the long term.

Women are fixed on the larger picture and tend to focus their attention inward only after they have bonded through telling their stories. Stories are vital to sharing and understanding the type of relationship they are building. Men, however, usually have little patience for stories, use few words, and just want to get to the bottom line of the sales process.

Only recently has the financial services industry begun to make progress toward developing a better understanding of the differences between how men and women approach a buying decision. However, all too often, men have no patience for listening to women's stories, dismiss the process, and, as a result, their female clients are offended.

Generations

The financial situations that women find themselves in vary as much due to changing social customs as with any other factor. At any one time, there are usually five different generations of women alive and their life experiences are usually very different. Consider, for example, the five generations of my family.

My grandmother had a "pin money" bank on her dresser. She would put coins in it that were given to her by my grandfather—this was her money that she could use to treat herself to a hat pin or personal item. Other that that, her generation of woman had no control of the household money.

The women of my mother's generation took great pride in keeping the home clean, baking, and cooking the family dinner (where the family would share the daily happenings of each member). She was given household money by my father and he had total control of all other aspects of the finances—this generation of woman relied on the husband to take care of them financially.

In my case, my mother was widowed at the age of fifty-five and forced to go to work (she chose cooking, for this is what she knew). She truly outlived her money, but the generation of her children took pride in helping their parents financially if needed.

My generation started a major change. Initially, we tried to be like Ozzie and Harriet (the ideal family of 1950s sitcoms). Many of us chose to do as our grandmothers and mothers did—keep a good home, serve family dinners, and participate in the PTA while our husbands provided for us financially and made all decisions regarding such things as life insurance needs and investments.

Some of my generation started careers outside the home after our children were established in school. Some women chose to start careers immediately after college. My generation of women wanted more financial independence and took pride in saving and paying for household needs. At that time, however, our financial needs were less complex. Groceries, for instance, were relatively less expensive than today and most people owned only one car and had little or no electronic equipment beyond a radio (and a television).

My daughter's generation was more accepting of careers outside the home. In fact, many of the women who chose to be full-time homemakers actually felt guilty about it (what a shame). Credit cards became a lifestyle and the cost of living was rising. Most people had two cars, and life was moving at a faster pace. Families had to fight for family time and tried to wedge family dinners in between taking children to sports activities, getting bigger homes, and buying more stuff. People were accumulating more credit card debt and found it more difficult to save. Company managed 401Ks and 403Bs forced many to save in spite of themselves (a good thing). People began to fear that there would be no social security to help them in their retirement.

My granddaughter's generation wants everything early and now. They are coping with the highest per capita cost of living so far in this country's history. This generation is more apt to move back home for financial security. It is saddled with heavy student loans at the same time that fewer jobs are available.

Regardless of what generation you are in, life has become more complex today. Each and every one of us has different dreams and needs. The Ozzie and Harriet generation may be faced with estate planning issues, long term care concerns, life insurance needs, legacy wants, and charitable giving to the community. They need to know that their financials are in order.

The Baby Boomer generation may be faced with having to save more money and cut back on spending. Insurance needs could be greater if assets are not enough to provide for their families. Single women are probably in the most difficult position of all. They not only have themselves to care for, but often have to cope with the concerns of their parents as well, without much help from other family members.

My granddaughter's generation had better get a handle on spending and start managing retirement plans—401Ks, 403Bs, etc. They need to understand the basic principles of financial responsibility. My advice to them is: Listen to your grandmother's words of wisdom.

— *Liz* —

When liz entered my office for the first time, she was thirty-eight—newly widowed with a preschool daughter.

Liz was referred by one of my clients who was her friend. Liz relayed how difficult it was for her to make decisions after her husband's death. She was interrupted in the evenings by solicitations from agents and brokers calling her as a result of her husband's obituary notice. Liz was very frightened about managing money, about finances, and about being both mom and dad to her daughter. She had a difficult time getting her life back in order and needed time to build trust and confidence.

We talked woman to woman and began developing a relationship; I could sense she was not yet ready for a detailed discussion about how to invest the sizable amount of insurance proceeds she received after her husband's death. She happily showed me pictures of their daughter, Roxanne, and carefully described the details of their life over the last months.

Liz explained, "I had Roxanne when I was thirty-four; neither Ron nor I had any other children previously." She proceeded to tell me of the joy they had with Roxanne who promised great happiness for both of them.

Only six months after Roxanne was born, Ron was diagnosed with lung cancer. It had metastasized to stage 4, and he was told he had between a month and two years to live; Ron was ill for four years. For the majority of that time, Ron remained strong and was able to handle many family responsibilities including the family finances.

Liz confided, "I knew I should get involved, and Ron tried to get me involved, but I had my hands full with a baby, a full-time job and the demands of his illness. I should have made myself develop a plan to learn about the family finances, in addition to attending to my priorities with Ron and Roxanne. I needed personal time for myself. Even before he became sick, he exclusively ran the household finances. I've never liked to hear women claim ignorance about family matters saying, 'My husband handles those things.' I knew better and wanted my life to be different, but I just never made it happen. In my first marriage, I was the one who handled everything and never liked it because it was stressful for me. When I married Ron, I felt lucky that we both shared similar values about maintaining good credit. The fact that Ron seemed so responsible and good at everything left me satisfied and complacent. His control of the finances made him feel he was participating in our family life during the illness. Therefore, while he was alive, I let him continue paying the bills, calling repairmen, and making decisions that I was not happy making. I didn't want to feel responsible for working outside the home, raising the child, taking care of all the domestic duties plus maintaining the household finances as well. As a result, I happily avoided the financial aspects."

Liz admitted, "Now I'm dragging myself, kicking and screaming, through all of this. Many times I wonder what Ron would be doing or how he would handle it. I'm not comfortable or confident about any of the advice I get. Learning how to deal with different business people, learning how to negotiate, and feeling comfortable enough to get three estimates for home repair projects should have been lessons learned much earlier than I did.

"Now, I'm also tired of hearing my friends and relatives tell me, after the fact, that I've paid too much. For instance, after getting pest control services, I had to get enough nerve to call the company back and say, 'Convince me that I didn't pay too much because my friends think that I did.' The person then explained how services and types of products vary depending on circumstances. After the explanation, I felt satisfied, but I want to feel satisfied *before* I buy the service, instead of justifying what I did afterwards. My friends admit that the pest control company I chose may make more visits to my house, but I still pay too much. To me the guarantees and the service are more important than the ultimate price. Because I do not feel that I have learned how to deal with these transactions, I am reluctant and not confident. Therefore, I'm delaying buying decisions.

"Also, as a widow I felt vulnerable when relatives wanted a share of the insurance proceeds following Ron's death. I'm an excellent example of not lending relatives money—any relative. Because I am very trusting, it is impossible for me to believe that someone would never pay a back a loan. I have a very trusted relative who currently owes me more than $20,000. I don't regret loaning the money, but I do regret not learning the parameters for such types of personal notes and not learning how to carry them out. Roxanne and I are doing all right, but the learning process has been painful for me at this stage in my life. We women should have a set of parameters for making these business transactions in light of the values and priorities we establish for ourselves. Then we need to stick to them and feel confident to handle these financial affairs on our own and master being responsible."

Just a year after being widowed, Liz was doing much better. She sold a rental house that was demanding too much of her time and was creating added expense. She updated her will and learned how mutual funds, annuities, investments and insurance work together to help shape her financial goals. Liz calls me frequently and visits to monitor the progress of her 401(k) portfolio and the growth of her mutual funds. She relies on our time together to continue her learning. She is feeling good about herself and her decisions. She has taken charge of her financial affairs; Liz has mastered *being responsible*.

STEP 1
Coordinating a Team of Advisors to Help Insure Success

— *Tom* —

Mike is a CPA whom I met at a meeting in Dallas. We were both involved with the financial services industry and had a mutual acquaintance. As we theoretically discussed our working relationship as professionals helping clients, it was obvious from Mike's conversation that we had begun a topic about which he felt quite strongly. He proceeded to tell me a story about Tom, a client of his. It demonstrates how fragmented most clients' planning is and how professionals should work together when providing service to clients.

Tom was quite pleased with his life as he got into the car. Mary, his wife, had just told him that she was pregnant with their fourth child, and the kids were excited about the onset of school. Tom's business was having a record year. The stock tip that he received three weeks ago from Bud, his broker, had generated a handsome profit that reminded Tom that Bud had wanted to discuss another stock trade.

As he turned onto the busy thoroughfare, Tom may have been wondering how many of these tips he would need to fund a college education for each of his four children. The stock figures and his sales calls for the day were on his mind as he discussed these issues on his cellular phone with Bud. Bud recalled stress in Tom's voice when he caught a glimpse of something in his mirror. That was probably the last glimpse he remembered. The truck driver later told police that Tom swerved as though he didn't expect anyone to be in his lane.

Tom had always stated that he was a salesman and did not understand all the implications of his financial decisions. That

was why he had an attorney to draft a will, a stock broker to purchase his stock trades, a financial professional, and an accountant
to ensure that his taxes were filed on time. Occasionally, Tom
would talk to his CPA about his will, or talk to his broker about tax
concerns and investments. Yes, Tom had all the professionals in
place to help him—but they never worked together on his behalf.

Tom was also aware that each of his professionals looked at
him through very different eyes. To the attorney, Tom was a business owner who came in every other year and who seemed to have
his business under control. To the stock broker, Tom was a
wheeler-dealer who was interested in any kind of investment that
could generate a quick return, yet he held other information about
personal finances close to his vest. To the financial professional,
Tom was the wild and crazy guy he knew in college. To his CPA,
Tom maintained a very low profile.

Tom's situation is common. He had presented himself as a
different person to each of those professionals whom he was trusting. Each accordingly developed different opinions about who
Tom was, and what his dreams and objectives were. Tom had a
group of professionals in place, but he had not developed a team
that communicated and planned together on his behalf.

People often use professionals in a limited fashion. In fact,
individuals often take more time to plan for the future of their business or their employees than they do their own family. So it was for
Tom. Instead of having a plan that all the professionals could implement as a team, Tom actually had no plan in place for the orderly
transfer of his business, to address his estate for his family, or to
help minimize the expense of probate and taxation after he died.

Tom's wife Mary would have to contend with issues related to
business continuation, succession, or sale. She would have to deal
with issues regarding Tom's estate. As a widow, Mary would be
administering these financial and legal matters for the first time. All
of this would be present along with the emotional loss of a loving
husband, her pregnancy, and the care of their children. When he
was alive, Tom assumed that he would always be available and
responsible to provide input to their financial and legal matters. In
addition to not reaping the maximum benefits from his profession-

als, Tom had not told them his expectations and wishes so that they could assist during a period of catastrophe and transition until Mary could reasonably assume more of the responsibilities.

Tom needed to have a general idea about what his and Mary's dreams were for the future. He needed to communicate those dreams and objectives to the professionals he was going to use as a team. He needed to solicit their opinions about how to implement plans to attain those objectives, and then he needed to monitor them and revise them if necessary. If Tom had only taken the time to get his professionals together in the same room to hear his dreams and objectives, he would have encouraged the professionals to develop a familiarity with each other that would improve communications among them. He would have better communicated with each of them about what his expectations were of them. He also would have begun bonds among them—bonds that would allow each of these professionals to feel as though they were part of a team—Tom and Mary's team. To get them together annually or semiannually nurtures their relationships as a team. It wouldn't have to be at the office; it could be done at a barbecue, at the pool or on the golf course.

Mike believes that as a CPA who works with the attorney and financial professional on a client's behalf, a team approach is necessary to understand the client's dreams and objectives and to focus on them. The members of the team are mutual resources that can be contacted about items of importance regarding the others' areas of expertise. For instance, as a CPA, Mike is concerned about whether or not clients have enough life or disability insurance. Such communication can help avert catastrophe for the client and the client's family. Working as a team allows each professional to perform to the best of his or her professional abilities as well as to be better focused on the client's needs. Every client deserves and should coordinate such a team approach.

Teamwork

Creating a professional team and coordinating ongoing communication can help build your confidence as well as give you emotional support that you are moving in the right direction to achieve your dreams. Your culture and lifestyle demands dictate the type of relationships you maintain with your team as well as how frequently you meet. Many of my clients meet me semiannually and bring along their attorney and CPA.

Rashinda, a divorced mother who recently began a small catering business explains, "It's not that I have transactions every six months; it's more that I want the financial professional, the CPA, and the attorney to be speaking to one another, and I want them to have me at the top of their mind. This way when there are changes in the tax law or investment strategies, I know I am in the loop. I only have so much time to keep up with things. It's a great way for me to learn gradually instead of feeling pressured and in the dark when I do need to purchase some products or make changes. I want them to know that I expect them all to be in sync with my personal and business finances. I used the attorney at real estate closing, my divorce, setting up a will and trust accounts for my children as well as the employee contracts and lease contracts when I began my business. I also needed my accountant involved with the tax issues. The team is quite clear about what I expect."

Rashinda is like many women who are "in charge" today. There is a raised level of consumer expectation about coordination of her total life plan; it demands a synchronized team approach. Also, even though you have accepted accountability and control for your own long-term financial goals, you are not entirely alone as long as you communicate with your professional team. Nor are you blindly following the crowd conversation you may hear at the office water cooler. Your financial professional can assist you with your protection and accumulation goals. Your CPA can help ensure that you are taking advantage of all available tax savings personally—and for your business. The attorney's counsel is necessary regarding drafting wills, trusts, and contracts.

From Tom's story, we can see how important it is for each team member to know the client's long-term goals and to update the other members of the professional team. The client needs to develop these relationships if they do not already exist. For example, if the financial professional feels that the client needs an overhead expense disability income policy, the CPA could provide valuable information regarding the growth of the business and cash flow. This will enable the financial professional to be thorough when applying for the insurance and to give the underwriters in-depth information about the business. Proactive communication is good because, if the client goes on disability claim, the financial professional and the CPA will be needed to help process the claim with the insurance company.

Personalities and expertise are needed to create a team of professionals with whom you are comfortable and who are comfortable working with each other. As Rashinda concludes, "I do not want three people going in separate directions. I want a coordinated team approach that is working together on my behalf."

Investment and Insurance Questions

You can address these key questions to your financial professional and registered representative.

- ♦ What type of life insurance should I have?
- ♦ How much life insurance do I need?
- ♦ What will happen to my insurance if I lose my job? How do I protect myself if this occurs?
- ♦ Where can I learn more about my insurance program?
- ♦ What is the difference between term, whole life, universal life, and variable life insurance?
- ♦ How does an annuity work?
- ♦ How do I know if I have the right kind of insurance?
- ♦ Is there anything I can do since I am no longer insurable?
- ♦ If I have no surviving relatives, what kind of insurance do I need?
- ♦ Should I have life insurance as a single woman without children?
- ♦ Do I need disability insurance since I have it at work?
- ♦ How much disability income protection should I have?
- ♦ Will my disability benefit be taxable at the time of my claim?
- ♦ How much money should I have as a reserve for emergencies?
- ♦ Should I pay more toward my mortgage monthly or invest in mutual funds instead?
- ♦ Should I pay off debt or invest more?
- ♦ What types of investments are suitable for me?

- How much can I contribute to my 401(k), 403(b) or IRA? Should I contribute more?
- When can I take income from my retirement plan?
- I have concerns regarding the size of my parents' estate and how much tax will be due when they die . . . What type of questions do I ask?
- What type of insurance should I have to take care of estate taxes?
- How do you know if insurance should be in a trust?
- Should I have a life insurance trust?
- What does asset protection mean?
- What is second-to-die insurance?
- Is the stability of my insurance company important?
- What does the rating of companies mean?

The Certified Public Accountant and Tax Issues

The CPA is involved with the client at least once a year for tax preparation and reviewing income, expenses, profit and loss statements to ensure that all information is properly documented on tax returns. The CPA is making sure the client takes advantage of ways to save taxes such as contributions to IRA, 401(k), 403(b), or contributions to other pension plans if available. The CPA should be astute to continued tax law changes and making sure proper deductions have been taken based on IRS rules. The CPA is often asked legal or insurance questions.

For example, the CPA has a client with high overhead in a business and is responsible for four children. The business has no disability program for the owner. The client asks if she should purchase a disability policy? How much does she need? How much would the premium be? The client may ask if $150,000 of life insurance enough? The client reveals that she is considering making her key employee a partner for the purpose of succession planning. She asks how the change should be structured? What type of legal documents are needed? Should there be insurance protection for this? If so, how much and what type?

This is a classic example of the client feeling comfortable asking the CPA the questions in the event he or she may not have a well-developed relationship with a financial professional or an attorney. These questions may arise because the client is introspective about life goals because it is tax time. The CPA should help the client by guiding the client to the financial professional or attorney. In the event the client does not have a financial professional or attorney, the CPA should coordinate a team approach so all of the client's goals can be addressed.

Tax Questions

As an individual or a business owner, the following are frequently asked questions that you can address to your CPA:

- ♦ What type of retirement program can I have?
- ♦ What will my capital gains tax be if I sell my home, farm, ranch or business?
- ♦ As my CPA do you do business valuation?
- ♦ Should I consider incorporating? If so, what type of corporation would you recommend?
- ♦ Can I pay my children a salary out of the business?
- ♦ Can I tax deduct my life insurance premium?
- ♦ Can I tax deduct my disability premium?
- ♦ Can I tax deduct my health insurance premium?
- ♦ Should I consider looking at employee benefits for my staff or updating my business equipment with the profits of my business?
- ♦ Am I making use of all available income tax deductions?

The Attorney and Legal Provisions

The attorney may specialize in tax planning, estate planning, or general practice such as family law, divorce, and custody issues. It is not likely that an attorney specializes in all of the above areas. For future financial strategies, the client would most likely seek out an attorney who specializes in tax planning, which would encompass business planning, estate planning, and personal tax planning.

This attorney specializes in implementation of contracts and legal documents such as business buy-sell agreements, setting up of corporations, many forms of trusts, wills, living wills and establishing various types of powers of attorney for the legal protection of the client.

For example, an attorney has been asked to draft a will, trust, and a family limited partnership for a client. The attorney needs to know the assets and liabilities of the client to complete family or business information, location of documents, and a complete analysis of the client's real estate and financial portfolio. Gathering and understanding of all the facts is necessary to properly draft the type of trust or legal documents best suited for the client based on the wants, needs, and desires of the client.

If the client or attorney chooses to bring in the team of specialists—in this case the CPA and the financial professional, the following would occur. If the CPA and financial professional have a long-term relationship with the client, their knowledge would be valuable to the attorney and substantial time and money could be saved for the client. The CPA would have full knowledge of the financial picture, regarding assets and liabilities, personal and business profit and loss, and real estate values. The financial professional also has information shared by the client. The financial professional could provide all insurance and investment statements including ownership and beneficiary assignment information and help the attorney diagnose the need and solution based on the goals of the client.

The relationship among your attorney, CPA, and financial professional can coordinate and advance your goals by providing: 1) shared knowledge of goals and personal and financial facts; 2) an integrated and properly designed long-term protection and accumulation program; 3) a network of trust and mutual respect, and ultimately; 4) a higher level of confidence regarding future planning.

Legal Questions

Here are common questions to address to your attorney:

+ What is power of attorney?
+ Do I need a trust? If so, what type of trust should I have?
+ I had my will done years ago does it need to be updated?
+ What is my estate value?

+ How much tax will be due on my estate when I die?
+ Should I consider a family limited partnership?
+ What type of buy-sell agreement should my partners and I have for our business?
+ What can I do to protect my special needs child?
+ Should I have a prenuptial agreement?
+ How does a living trust work?
+ How does a living will work?
+ What type of corporation should I have? What is the difference between a C-corporation and an S-corporation?

How the Team Works Together

As a service to my clients, I have cultivated relationships with a number of attorneys and CPAs over the years. The most typical situation is that the tax planning attorneys review the needs of their clients and observe that clients are underinsured or question if the policies are designed correctly for the intended purpose. The CPAs or attorneys request that I meet with clients either at their office or my business setting to discuss their insurance program. I am provided policies and all information pertaining to the coverage, why insurance was originally purchased, its objective, and how it has been updated.

We will organize the portfolio and prepare a completed spread sheet listing the name of the company, contract number, current cash value, outstanding loans, owner and beneficiary of the policies, and premium amount. This is provided to the client, the attorney, and the CPA in addition to an analysis and suggestions on how to coordinate additional coverage if needed in the present portfolio.

For my own clients, I coordinate a meeting with either an attorney or a CPA. They provide one free hour consulting at my office if my clients are in need of estate or tax planning. This saves the client from visiting additional offices and helps the client focus on long-term goals while allowing the team of specialists to communicate appropriate strategies based on the need. I believe the financial professional should be the coordinator in providing information to the advisors along with coordinating meeting times

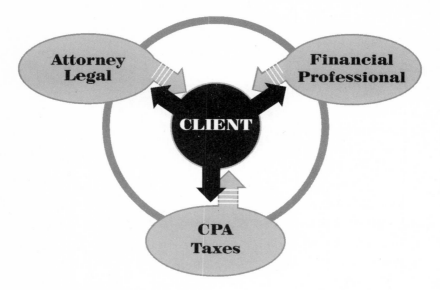

and places. Once the team is in place, annual reviews and ongoing needs and strategies can be easily recommended for the client.

Many professionals have received interdisciplinary training in complementary areas and are much sought after. A few examples are:

- ♦ CPA
- ♦ Attorney
- ♦ Financial Professional

There are a variety of possibilities for such credentials and training across legal, accounting, insurance and investment disciplines. The most important concept for you to realize is that *you do not want one professional "doing it all" for you.* The legal, tax accounting, insurance, and investment worlds are extremely complex and various areas of specialty require years of continuing education and experience. As a result of using many professionals for guidance, *it is imperative that you set the stage to have them working as a coordinated team on your behalf.*

— David —

In 1991, I chose to invite local attorneys, CPAs, and financial planners to my office for a seminar on insurance needs analysis and on the importance of a properly designed financial program encompassing health insurance, disability income insurance, life insurance, pension planning, and estate planning.

David was one of many attorneys who came to the session. As he was leaving, he asked if I would work with him regarding his own business and personal insurance needs. Later, when I arrived at his office, I received a warm welcome from his staff. His office setting was professional and inviting. I felt honored to be working with such a well-respected attorney who was also quite humble.

We discussed his dreams and what he wanted to accomplish. I left the appointment with a box full of assorted papers, such as insurance contracts, retirement statements, mutual fund balances, and the like, which he had accumulated over the years.

My promise to David was that I would organize all his financial papers and return them on my next visit. I would organize his formal files according to: insurance, retirement, business, pension, and estate needs; plus each contract or policy would be accompanied with a full explanation.

David is a very giving person who lives his life for his wife and two children; he is active in the community and in his church. His overall desire is to create a financial legacy for all those people who are important to him. As I unraveled all of his insurance policies, I soon discovered that he had purchased various types of life insurance from different agents. But it was apparent that none of these agents had taken the time to properly design a total financial program based on David's income, expenses, wants, needs, and desires for his family. The entire box of papers did not contain any analysis of David's income relative to his expenses; therefore, it was difficult to determine whether David's policies and contracts would adequately cover his family income needs in the event of his death.

David recalls, "I admit that I had purchased insurance policies from assorted agents without too much thought being given as to specific overall needs. The coordination of my life, health and disability insurance programs transformed my efforts from a helter-skelter, hodgepodge mess into a coherent and coordinated program. Other agents had asked about current financial situation, debts, income and assets, but Mary wanted to know about my dreams for myself and my family. I related that I wanted to not only pay off debts at my death, but also to leave my family with enough money to cover living expenses, college and a legacy for future generations."

When we designed David's insurance program, I recommended that he be personally and actively involved in the process. I took the time to teach him how the different types of products would work for him and how they would provide solutions to what he wanted to accomplish financially. David's joint involvement and input made it very easy for us to make the most of this planning process. As we proceeded through the entire process, David explained that many of his clients had need of this type of thorough review and analysis to better understand their own financial affairs.

David had a business partner who died unexpectedly. There was no insurance to pay off debts in the event that one partner died prematurely. Because David had cosigned the loans, he was left to single-handedly pay off all the bank notes over time.

When David purchased disability income protection, he gained confidence; that in turn enabled him to muster all his financial resources to pay off debt. He remembers, "I was better able to intensely focus financial resources on paying off the bank notes, because I knew that my insurance would take care of my family if I died prematurely." By purchasing an individual disability income policy, David took the first step to protect his income earning potential in the event that he became disabled and qualified for benefits. Also, if David became disabled, he would still need to cover the expenses associated with running his law practice; therefore, he applied for an additional *business overhead disability income* insurance policy.

David was satisfied with this process for analyzing and organizing his financial affairs. I agreed to perform an insurance needs analysis as well as help his clients understand how insurance, pensions, and investments work together. As a result, he agreed that I could refer my clients to him for consultation on wills and trust agreements.

This team concept between a financial professional and an attorney has been an asset to our clients. David's clients' insurance programs are now coordinated with their overall financial program and estate planning, and my clients have properly drafted wills and trust agreements.

Life experiences such as divorce, custody, or settling the estates of loved ones affect us; but these do not affect only one segment of our lives. People working with attorneys to create prenuptial agreements, to settle divorce, or to handle estate issues have many questions about the impact that such legal milestones have on their financial life as well. As an attorney, David also ensured that his statutory power of attorney, health care power of attorney and a living will were in order. Ideally, your attorney and financial professional should work together for the benefit of you and your family.

David's goal is to leave a legacy by having his insurance program in order based on his dreams. His desire is that when he dies, "I want [Mary] to show my family just how much I loved them when she delivers a check sufficient to cover all of their financial concerns. Buying life insurance is one of the ultimate acts of love and unselfishness. With insurance comes the peace of mind that your family will be taken care of financially. The love that we thrive on and share will continue to sustain them after I die."

STEP 2
Selecting Your Professional Advisors

Finding a Financial Professional

Once you understand the value of coordinating a professional team, your next task becomes selecting your professionals.

From working with my clients, it seems that the most common pattern for people taking the first steps in protecting their assets is to begin with insurance. Indeed, many people do not even think of insurance as part of their future planning process. They must select car insurance in their teens, then renter's insurance, perhaps accident insurance when they fly, and home insurance. If they are employed by a corporation, they become introduced to the world of medical insurance, other employee benefits, and retirement planning. At this stage in life, most of their financial awareness revolves around insurance and protection needs. As they advance through marriage and business interests on their journey through life, they eventually build relationships with a CPA and an attorney. This sequence is not the same for everyone, but it is one shared by a majority of women whom I serve in my practice.

For most, purchasing insurance through an agent is their initiation into the financial world. This initiation has been one where many women have been frustrated and frightened.

Women often tell me that they work with many professionals for separate purposes, yet no one coordinates their total financial picture. I see this approach as being like inviting people to a pot luck supper at your home. There are many interesting alternatives brought in to choose from, yet there is not necessarily a coordinated nutritional balance. The spontaneity of a pot luck supper may be fun for the weekend, but a daily diet wouldn't be healthy. In the same way, an uncoordinated smorgasbord of financial products and professionals isn't necessarily the best diet for the long-term. Ultimately, women buyers should demand that all of their financial vehicles and services be coordinated to the greatest extent possible. It is important that planning for the future be in the hands of someone who knows and understands how to coordinate separate health, disability income, and life insurance protection as well as annuities, stocks, bonds, mutual funds, and various other investments. In addition, it is important to recognize risks to property that have accumulated. Financial professionals should identify and recommend that sufficient amounts of automobile, homeowners, or renters insurance be purchased to protect against liability.

The premise of my practice is that a very good financial professional can and should be the catalyst to help you coordinate a professional team and suggest when it is time for you to seek counsel and begin establishing these other key relationships necessary for your future financial growth and wealth accumulation.

When you begin your planning, you should choose your financial professional, CPA and/or attorney as carefully as you would select a life partner. Ideally, the relationship should grow more fulfilling over time.

Now let's look at a process that will help you find and select a financial professional.

Friends and Referrals

Women ask me how they can ensure that the financial professional they chose is right for them. Where can they find someone for the long term? If I were to choose a financial professional today, I would spend a great deal of time talking with personal friends. Question friends whom you believe to be astute regarding the financial marketplace or those who seem to be actively involved in saving and planning. Their responses may be complete and helpful. Spend time asking some key questions:

♦ Are they happy with their present financial professional? Why or why not?
  You are looking for a quick response here. If it takes your friends time to answer this one, the financial professional probably isn't a key player in their financial decisions.

♦ What specifically has their financial professional accomplished for them?

Here again, you are looking for a quick and concise answer. You want to hear responses like, "The financial professional put me on a program to help fund my children's education" or ". . . a program that can provide me with a certain monthly income when I retire." Responses such as these indicate two important principles: first, that the financial professional identified and created a strategy for your friends' needs; and secondly, that the financial professional presented the sale in such a manner that your friends easily understand. If you hear, "The financial professional sold me a life insurance policy," that is not a stellar response. It indicates that your friends' needs may not have been uncovered and that there may be little, if any, connection between something your friends bought and dreams they have for the future.

♦ Does their financial professional have a support staff that assists with service questions?

Financial professionals earn their living by new sales. Successful financial professionals have made an investment in hiring staff to provide service to each client on a timely basis. A financial professional with staff is truly running a business and is more likely to be responsive. It also means that the financial professional may have other professional associates with complementary expertise available easily to you.

♦ What does their financial professional specialize in?

You are looking for an answer that is more specific than "insurance" or "investments" or "brokerage." If a financial professional does not totally disclose areas of expertise to clients, how do you know what you are buying? Think of it this way, you wouldn't hire someone who advertised that they did home repairs if you specifically needed an electrician, a plumber, or a roofer. You would have no professional guarantee that the house wouldn't burn, or the pipes and the roof wouldn't leak.

♦ Is their financial professional one who handles multiple lines of business such as life, health, and disability income protection?

Ultimately, the goal is coordination of all of your financial affairs. This means that eventually you will also be dealing with a CPA and an attorney. The more tasks that your financial professional has experience in, the simpler it will be to coordinate your team.

♦ Is their financial professional building a relationship with them over time by sending newsletters, conducting periodic reviews of their program, or maintaining ongoing correspondence?
You are looking for an answer that indicates that the financial professional is willing and able to invest in a long-term relationship.

♦ Do they receive quarterly or annual review updates?
The way of life is change. You want to find a financial professional who provides annual or biannual reviews to help ensure that the coverage you have today meets your needs as the value of the dollar changes and as your family and income needs change.

♦ Does the financial professional invite them to attend educational seminars of interest?
This will demonstrate whether or not the financial professional keeps up with changes in the industry and willingly seeks to make clients more knowledgeable.

♦ What is it that really stands out about the service their financial professional provides?
A quick response is what you are looking for here. If your friends need to think long and hard about this question, then it is doubtful that a relationship has been built. Desirable answers are: the financial professional is easy to understand, or the financial professional teaches me until I understand everything, or the financial professional is always there for me.

♦ What character traits have they seen to be outstanding in their financial professional?
"Understanding," "trustworthy," "caring," and "sympathetic" are honorable responses here. "Drives a sporty car" may not be the answer you are looking for unless you are open for a ride.

Ask your friends all of these questions and ask if they conducted an interview with the prospective financial professional. Ultimately, determine what mattered in their final selection.

By Telephone Book or Directory

If your questions to friends leave you feeling that you've not discovered what you're looking for, and if you've not yet established an ongoing relationship with a CPA or attorney who can refer you to a reputable financial professional, working from a telephone book can tell a big story about a financial professional. First of all, if you've been given a referral on a financial professional who's not listed in any way, it could mean that the financial professional is new in the business, hasn't built a name yet, or is new in the area. The financial professional may work within a large *career agency* sales office, but even if this is the case, the agency will often also have a phone number listed for the individual financial professional.

If you are trying to find a financial professional by looking in a telephone book or directory, look for specialty areas. These are based on your interest. For example under the "physicians" in the telephone book, you'll find "internal medicine," "family practice," and "pediatrics" as categories.

In your telephone book, financial professionals are listed by area of specialty as well. You want to refer to auto and homeowners insurance, known in the trade as property-casualty, or life, health, and disability income insurance. Some financial professionals are registered representatives who have also received advanced education or degrees and are licensed to sell variable annuities and mutual fund investments. Investigate about what services and types of insurance the financial professional advertises in the yellow pages. As a woman, you may prefer working with a woman, just as many of us prefer doing business with a physician or attorney who is a woman.

If more than one financial professional is recommended, it's time to start the interviewing process yourself. If there is to be good chemistry between you and the professional you are choosing, I suggest you do your homework and begin an interviewing process. Selection by referrals is usually best. If you are pleased with your CPA or attorney, ask for a reference for a financial professional. That's always a win-win method because, ultimately, if your planning is to serve your needs, your attorney, CPA and financial professional should and will inevitably work as a team—as you, your family, and/or your business mature.

STEP 3
Interviewing to Find the Right Match for You

The Right Stuff

Your next step is to begin an interviewing process to find a financial professional who is right for you. Credentials and experience of the financial professional are important. However, your comfort level is even more important—especially for women buyers. I cannot stress enough the importance of experiencing this essential step.

By interviewing several potential financial professionals, you communicate and establish a respect for yourself; but equally important is the confidence this process gives you. Conducting interviews reaffirms that you are the prime mover and that you are actively taking charge of your financial affairs. If you are skeptical or believe that you can skip this step, approach it as you would a major purchase. You would not buy a car or a home without considerable discussion and review of the benefits and drawbacks of each option available to you. The relationship you develop should be a long-term commitment; your choice needs to be one with which you are happy and satisfied.

Usually you shouldn't need to interview more than two or three prospective financial professionals. Visit their offices to see what type of business environments they have each created. Tell them that you are interviewing for a financial professional and would like to visit and ask some questions before you make a final selection. Ask the following:

♦ What lines of business is the financial professional licensed to sell?
State departments of insurance require that all individuals selling life insurance be licensed; this also applies to individuals selling property and casualty insurance as well as health insur-

ance. In addition to having state licenses, financial professionals who sell securities products, variable annuities, and variable life insurance (which rely on a variety of risks and rewards due to their investment in stocks and bonds) must be appropriately licensed with a broker/ dealer who is registered with NASD. Contact your state insurance department if you have any questions about the licensing status of an financial professional.

♦ If a financial professional has a limited area of specialization, you will need to work with several people to cover all of your requirements. For example, if you have a need for any insurance—life, auto and homeowners, health, and disability income—or investments, it is not likely that one financial professional typically handles all. If this is the case, you can ask if the financial professional has supplementary staff associates or a network of other financial professionals.

♦ Does the financial professional work with individuals and families, or small businesses, or professionals?

This question enables you to understand the scope of the financial professional's practice. It is doubtful that a financial professional who works only in the family market will be able to assist you if you are starting a business or plan to be involved in a business in the near future.

♦ Does the financial professional have staff?

An established financial professional is most likely aligned with other financial professionals and can refer you to them for specialty areas. It is rare for one financial professional to keep up continued education in all areas; therefore, a financial professional will often hire a staff of specialists to assist you. As a result, all of your auto, homeowners, disability income, and life insurance needs can be coordinated. Also, having a staff to handle service calls means that there is always someone to handle your service needs and intercede with the insurance company on your behalf. Your service requests are more likely to be handled promptly if there is staff. You want to determine how readily available the financial professional is to you if you are in need. Ask how quickly your call will be returned—in an hour, in a day, in two days?

♦ How many years has the financial professional been in business?

The first four years are considered critical in the insurance business because this time is often the hardest period in a financial professional's career; it's the time when the financial professional is most likely to leave the business. A financial professional who has weathered these early years is more likely to be committed to the career for the long-term.

♦ What would happen to my insurance and investments if the financial professional becomes disabled or dies?

It should be a real concern for you if something happens to the financial professional. This is a legitimate question. Many financial professionals have prepared successor programs where a younger financial professional is planning to buy the senior financial professional's business or take over the practice. By the same token, a financial professional with twenty years or more in the business may be ready to retire or change careers. If you select an older seasoned financial professional, ask him or her if there is a business succession arrangement in place to ensure continuity of service to you. You want someone who knows you, to be there as you grow older and your needs change. As a client, you need to know that the company is always behind the scene and maintaining permanent records of your account. It is important to remember that the insurer will be obligated to honor the terms of the insurance contract even if the financial professional is unable to continue to serve your needs.

Chemistry Quiz

The answers to the questions you've asked in the interview will help you judge whether or not the financial professional you have selected has the fundamental credentials and experience to provide you sound advice. Now you must listen to your heart and ask yourself if you could trust whom you've selected and consider that person to *be among your best friends*. Each one of us has different needs. But if you feel the need to be taught, look for a person who is willing to take time to teach you. Learning from a financial professional willing to take the time to explain the hows and whys of insurance and investment products helps women to gain confidence and to enjoy the journey to attain dreams and financial goals.

Ultimately, try to imagine this. Picture yourself in a hospital; you have just been told you have cancer. You are frightened and need a friend who can take over processing a claim—someone who will be available to family members regarding financial needs and questions. You want someone willing to take time to be there as your friend because the best financial professional is a friend for life.

When you are interviewing potential financial professionals, sometimes your intuition immediately tells you if the chemistry is right or wrong. You need to assess the chemistry of the individual with whom you'll be working. You need to find someone you are comfortable with socioeconomically. You need to feel that you have something in common with this financial professional. As a financial professional, I'm a wife, mother, grandmother, sister, and a business owner. Many of my women clients can relate to this; we share similar experiences. I can talk about many problems and pose many strategies because I've lived through many of the problems myself. And I can share solutions that have worked. This provides a great deal of comfort to my clients.

If you are feeling angry over the past—following the death of a loved one, divorce, loss of income, or financial failure—your financial professional should be someone who will understand your anger and who will care enough to help you get excited about your future by showing you options to best fit your financial capabilities and goals. Maybe you've gone through a divorce, and you do not feel that the settlement was fair to you. Maybe you were a homemaker until your divorce; afterwards, for the first time in your life, you had to enter the working world. Drastic changes in lifestyle can build resentments. You may want to share all of these inner feelings. I have been told by many women that they find it easier to share such concerns with another woman because she will listen.

Eventually, you reach a point in life when you realize it's time to be independent and accountable for the financial affairs that affect your life rather than rely solely on the information provided by your father, husband, boyfriend, children or employer. Women are emerging to take responsibility for their own financial affairs. That means their insurance and investment planning as well as buying a car or home. Ultimately, if there is insufficient planning done for our future, we have no one to blame but ourselves; we cannot blame someone else for negligence on our behalf. Remember, it is an actuarially based fact that women live several years longer than men. Therefore, if you are married, you should be proactive in the planning strategies that will most likely support you after your husband is gone.

Also, when selecting the financial professional with the right emotional match for you, ask yourself if you are comfortable with a low-key approach or respond positively to a hard sell. There are different styles of individuals in this world. Some are more low key—there to help you when you need it but not repeatedly calling. However, if you are a person who needs to be called, encouraged, and reminded, then you will need a financial professional whose staff can work this way for you. The financial professional will let you know whether the staff provides proactive service or reactive service.

STEP 4
Identifying Unethical Behavior

The Good, the Bad and the Ugly

By working with women clients over the years, I've learned that *the ethics, values, and integrity of the financial professional and the company are top priorities in women's decisions to buy*. Men I've worked with seem to place more value on competitive price and/or product when making a buying decision. This further distinguishes how men generally purchase and whether or not women will purchase at all.

I've known a woman to leave a six-figure salary because the ethical and moral conditions of a company, its leadership, and the job forced her to compromise personal integrity. Women may leave relationships if ethics and moral trust have been breached with their partners.

If situations or behaviors are unethical, some people may tend to be silent about them, detaching themselves from the problem. Most women in a relationship cringe at the memory of when their partners take a vow of silence and avoid discussing anything with them—as if distancing eliminates accountability for any inappropriate conduct, or if by discussing the issues, he believes that he has lost power and control. A woman wants to be open and direct. She wants to communicate with him and lay all the cards on the table. She wants to see him demonstrate by his speech and actions that his values are the same as her values. If there is silence or no demonstration of shared values, it may be difficult for her to develop trust over time.

Women generally carry this attitude into business. I have found that women not only demand that the financial professional and the company they choose have ethics and integrity, but also that a definite communication and demonstration of these values exists. More and more, women are demanding that these values be communicated on an ongoing basis.

When it comes to the sale of financial products, there are many ugly stories. The news media seek these with a pious vengeance. Past insurance debacles in Pennsylvania, Florida, and Texas regarding financial professional misrepresentations have resulted in a renewed emphasis on and enforcement of professional ethics. Companies have always monitored their financial professionals and registered representatives. However, during the last decades, corporate officers who serve on the American Council on Life Insurance have voluntarily heightened the internal monitoring of their ranks.

Companies are imposing and enforcing even more stringent guidelines and procedures that individual financial professionals must follow regarding the advertising, description, and sale of insurance products, mutual funds, and securities to the consumer. Companies require that any and all marketing materials used by financial professionals be formally approved to ensure conformity with legal, regulatory, and compliance guidelines; this is being monitored in local sales offices, regional offices, and the corporate headquarters.

All financial professionals should demonstrate ethics and integrity, and my hope is that you will not encounter any unethical situations regarding your insurance or financial program. Here are some sales practices that can serve as red flags for you. These are all considered unethical in the insurance industry because the end result of the action can be harmful to the client over the long term.

- ◆ Be wary if a financial professional offers to give you money as an incentive to buy a product. This is known as rebating, and it is illegal in almost all instances (check your state law).
- ◆ Be wary if a financial professional tells you about a great new product that would be better for you if you cashed in your old policy.
- ◆ Be wary if a financial professional tells you that you can use the dividends or values in one policy to buy a new policy.

+ Be wary if a financial professional collects a second premium payment and you still do not have a written policy for your files.

+ Be wary if a financial professional delivers a policy to you that is different than your understanding of what you purchased.

+ Be wary if a financial professional takes a payment from you in cash.

+ Be wary if a financial professional takes a payment without completing a detailed written or computer automated application.

+ Be wary if a financial professional asks for a payment and asks that you make the bank check payable to a name other than the name of the insurance company that is seen on the printed materials you are given.

+ Be wary if a financial professional wants to replace an existing insurance policy while taking an application for new coverage. As a consumer, you should request that the financial professional obtain from your company written information that shows the death benefit, present cash value, and premium. The financial professional attempting to replace your coverage should also obtain future values of your present contract. A financial professional should not discuss replacement under any condition whatsoever without this information. In many instances, it is not in the best interests of the insured to replace one life insurance policy with another. However, should you believe you want to do so, make certain you have all the facts.

The insurance industry isn't the only financial services sector that has experienced ethics violations. The banking industry and the securities industry have suffered from trustees who have embezzled or lost client's money through unsound or speculative investments that were inappropriate for the client's needs and risk tolerance. To help protect yourself you should:

+ Make sure your professional completes a risk tolerance questionnaire. She or he should explain and review it with you prior to making investment decisions. This can help determine whether your investment portfolio is diversified according to your tolerance for the different risks associated with goals that range from conservative to aggressive.

♦ Be diligent in requesting and reviewing frequent performance statements. Be personally responsible for reading and understanding how to calculate the present value of your portfolio.

Replacement

Replacement of insurance policies is a serious issue—for the industry and for you as a consumer. You could have extensive debates with actuaries about the values of your policies, but as a consumer you are generally better off to coordinate your insurance program around what you presently have rather than to seek replacement. If you are adamant and feel that, for some reason, you need to replace a policy, the financial professional has the responsibility of explaining the negative consequences for that action. The financial professional also has the responsibility of showing you how your current policy is performing.

There is a philosophy in the marketplace that states "buy term and invest the difference." Financial professionals for companies advocating this philosophy accomplish this tactic with a strategy that involves replacing people's whole life insurance policies that have been in force for many years and carry substantial cash value. It is not wise to fall for this type of sale (see Jeanne's story).

Replacement is one of the most controversial ethical and legal issues in the insurance and investment industries. Often the companies and financial professionals that use replacement sales tactics attempt to cash in old whole life policies and use the money for other purposes. They satisfy insurance needs with temporary term insurance and place the extra money in mutual funds. The idea is that the investment portfolio will hypothetically grow so much in twenty years—or whatever the term was—that the insurance won't be needed anymore. If anyone could predict that they won't die or become uninsurable within that period of time, it could be a valid idea. However, in reality, such a strategy often turns out to be tragic for the consumer. In many cases, it will not solve the long-term needs that most people have because the term insurance may lapse or be too expensive to maintain as the insured gets older.

Many women have told me that husbands have been lured into this trap with the prospects of attractive and lucrative mutual fund returns. The wife who thinks her husband has everything under control is often devastated to find that he had succumbed to a replacement strategy and there is now no insurance at all, and the mutual funds he bought instead didn't perform as well as he thought they would.

Strategy Turned Tragedy

Replacement in order to buy term and invest the difference has turned to tragedy for several of my clients. One forty-year-old gentleman cashed in his existing whole life policies to purchase term insurance from another company five years ago. He has since lost his insurability due to a heart attack and degenerating condition, and he will probably never get insurance again. The financial professional replaced $100,000 of whole life coverage with $75,000 of twenty-year term insurance. When the whole life policy was fifteen years old, if the original dividend scale had been maintained, the policy should have had enough cash value accumulated in it to offset the premium payments.

The term insurance that he bought was a twenty-year level term. That means that his premium would stay the same for twenty years and the death benefit would never be more than $75,000— but only for that twenty-year period, or when he becomes sixty years old. Most level term policies still provide coverage after the initial term, just at a higher premium; so this may be misleading.

An alternate strategy would have been to keep his whole life policy in force and (so long as the dividends were sufficient to continue to offset the premium payments) use the same premium amount to purchase mutual funds. Here are the potential consequences of the gamble he made:

- If he lives longer than age sixty and is uninsurable, the level term policy will allow continued coverage but at a premium that could be substantially higher.
- If he lives beyond age sixty, he will have forfeited the potential cash value built up in his original whole life policy that could have provided him with living benefits and monthly supplemental income during his retirement years.

♦ If he lives to age sixty and tries to purchase insurance (for the purpose of helping to fund a buy-sell agreement on a business or additional insurance for his family, or to help pay estate taxes), he may not be able to because he may be uninsurable due to his heart attack.

♦ If he dies before age sixty, his family receives less insurance. Plus, the mutual funds he purchased may not have grown enough to compensate for the shortfall.

Replacing one policy with another means that you are starting over. You are starting over at an older age and generally at higher premiums, but the financial professional who replaced your policy receives a new commission for the sale. Replacement is often only to the benefit of the financial professional who is doing the replacement and is often at considerable cost and consequence to the consumer.

Unethical sales practices in the area of replacement are simple to counter and defend against. Just say no!

Providing Annual Service and Teaching

In addition to replacement, there are other undesirable practices that deal with ways of selling women financial products. They are not illegal, but I am impassioned about them. I believe these practices extend the issue of what is appropriate when selling to women. I propose the following:

♦ It is inappropriate to sell financial products based on a transaction emphasizing price and product without relating them to a basic fact-finding discussion of income, expenses, wants, needs, and desires for the future.

♦ It is inappropriate to sell financial products to women with any approach other than an approach that teaches women through a relationship that builds her knowledge and confidence over time.

One common ugly experience that clients have relayed occurs when women are being talked to in a manner that assumes they know all the definitions of financial jargon rather than in a manner that focuses on teaching. You might have had this experience in the past; it is a nightmare that women don't easily forget. The moment it happens again, it should send up red flags that working with this financial professional isn't for you.

Women should demand to understand every aspect of a purchase. The purchase of a refrigerator provides an analogy. Most women are not concerned about the motor size, but women are concerned about the shelf space, freezer size, and self-defrosting unit. Capacity or function take priority over motor size. As buyers, women want to see more than one size or style and maybe more than one manufacturer. Typically, when women have an experience of buying a product that turns out to be unsuitable, it results from having minimal information or from being shown only one product.

Regarding insurance, often the frustration results when a relationship has not been developed (or will never develop) between the financial professional and the woman buyer. The financial professional emphasizes price or product, but never understands truly what her goals are for her program. Making this type of "transaction" sale to a woman buyer is inappropriate because it is a tactic based on bottom-line product selling rather than in-depth client needs analysis, education, and ongoing client service over time.

The ability to learn by asking questions is crucial. No woman wants to deal with someone who is not willing to answer questions that she believes are relevant and sincere. In terms of selling financial services products to women, this involves avoiding financial jargon, teaching women at their level of understanding, and providing strategies designed to achieve their goals in terms they can understand. It means being responsible for ongoing service after the sale.

Another issue of utmost importance is the consequence of not providing annual service. The monetary value of the dollar changes as currency values change. Lifestyles change. Circumstances and responsibilities in family life change. Dependents change. Laws change. There are numerous stories about the consequences that result when beneficiaries are not updated.

STEP 5
Knowing What You Want

— Lahonda —

I remember what a striking couple Lahonda and Ronny were. They were both impeccably groomed. Ronny's shirt was hand ironed and his boots newly polished. Lahonda was vibrant in her crisp cotton slacks and plaid blouse; she wore perfectly tailored clothes of fabrics that demanded much attention to look freshly pressed. Her nails were newly manicured, and her brown hair was salon styled and curled to perfection. Every detail indicated that she and Ronny took special time to look their best and that great care was taken to prepare for the visit to my office. There was a look of firm resolve on her face.

She had an eternal smile, and she opened her arms to give me a huge hug the moment she entered my office. She wheeled in Ronny, who was disabled with multiple sclerosis. During our chat, it became easy to see that she was happy to have made the trip with her husband and happy to discuss their concerns. As I introduced Ronny and Lahonda to what services I would provide them, it was obvious that Lahonda was directing the conversation. Ronny sat relaxed in his wheel chair while Lahonda told me their story; she was forty-one that Tuesday.

She explained that Ronny had lived with MS for more than twenty years, and the severity of his condition required her strictest attention daily. Their son, Stephen, was eighteen years old.

Lahonda had been battling cancer for three years and was in remission. She had solid hopes for the future. She worked a part-time job and was thankful for its flexible hours that enabled her to attend to Ronny.

Lahonda had two main concerns. First, she wanted to totally understand their current life insurance coverage. She was proud that she had purchased considerable individual whole life insurance when she was in her mid-thirties. She had planned to purchase more, but she never thought she would become uninsurable at an early age. Lahonda sadly admitted, "You know Mary, a person can never ever know when they may lose their insurability; then it's too late." She wanted to know the current values of her policies and the benefits that would be left for Ronny and Stephen.

Second, because Lahonda and Ronny both had serious diseases and poor prognoses for the future, they had genetic concerns about Stephen's ability to obtain his own life insurance because of his parents' poor health. Stephen's future insurability as he became older was a passionate concern for Lahonda. She adamantly indicated that she wanted Stephen to have $350,000 of life insurance of his own if possible. He had been a loving and helpful son and was in excellent health at that time. Remembering that Ronny was only twenty-seven years old when he contacted MS, Lahonda felt extreme urgency to help her son obtain insurance while he was young and healthy.

We proceeded to review their policies, monthly expenses, and any available assets. It was apparent they lived a lifestyle without debt, saved monthly, and enjoyed financial security in spite of their daily challenges. Through the entire process, Lahonda was strong and focused on her family's needs. As I reviewed their coverage, Lahonda would smile at Ronny. With his dark sparkling eyes, he returned her smile and occasionally embraced her arm as if he were really proud of what she had done. From their many years of struggle, a love and closeness emanated between them that I have witnessed only rarely in couples.

She asked that I explain differences, benefits, and drawbacks of both cash value and term life insurance; she was not certain about these. After considering all options, Lahonda confidently indicated that she preferred permanent insurance over term, because she wanted Stephen to have uninterrupted life insurance for the rest of his life. This was his mother's and father's bequest and legacy to him.

That meeting with Lahonda and Ronny was an inspiration about the power of life insurance. For Lahonda, it was clear that she was motivated by love to obtain insurance for Stephen, but she was also fearful of not having enough insurance on her own life in order to provide daily care for Ronny in the event she predeceased him. When they left my office that day, Ronny thanked me, and Lahonda was quick to offer another hug as she smiled an intense sigh of relief.

We applied for the coverage on Stephen as they wished. A few weeks later, I delivered their gift to their son—a $350,000 policy. As Lahonda wrote the check for the annual premium, her eyes gazed intently at Ronny. She said, "Promise me, Ronny, that if anything happens to me, you will always make sure this policy is secure. When Stephen is out of college and working, he can assume the payments on his own." Ronny took her hand in his and smiled at her affirming his vow that he would carry out her wishes.

Over the next few months, Lahonda called to keep me updated about what was happening with her family. In October, she notified me that her cancer returned and was moving very fast. She had been experiencing severe headaches and did not know how long she could communicate; her doctors were medicating her severely. We cried because we both knew we were losing a special relationship, and she was losing the battle. The last time I spoke with her, she reiterated how she appreciated the work we did together and asked if I would please stay in touch with Ronny and Stephen. Again indicating that she wished she had more life insurance to leave to her family, she said, "Mary, be proud of what you do, and tell my story whenever you feel a need so that it may help other women."

Lahonda died in December 1994, leaving Stephen and Ronny to carry on—with the memory of her eternal smile.

Wants, Needs and Desires

Understanding the happy times as well as the obstacles and shattered dreams of my clients has been a major part of building the relationships we have. Relationship building with a financial professional ought to feel comfortable and open enough for you to honestly share or vent your fears. It should be as I remember when talking to my guardian angel as a child; my angel was someone who would know my worst fears, someone who would help me out of a mess and stay on my side forever.

If your relationship with your financial professional does not feel that way, then it will never stand the test of time. Perhaps you should continue your search. As consumers, American women have the benefits of choice to their advantage. There are hundreds of life insurance companies and financial services companies with thousands of financial professionals available, so your chances of interviewing and selecting a professional who's right for you are very good.

In her best-selling book, *The Popcorn Report*, futurist Faith Popcorn makes three distinctions in consumer's motivations for buying. These are to satisfy wants, needs, and desires. Each rests on a continuum from providing basic necessities through satisfying self-actualization goals.

Here are a few examples. If women are to secure their financial independence in America today, I consider food, clothing, shelter, transportation, education, and retirement to be basic needs. Desires are the emotional conditions that women define as important to their sense of success or self-actualization. Wants are the means to attain these ends. You may *desire to* educate your children through college, to own a business, to have a second vacation home, to buy a boat, or to attain financial independence. In order to achieve these desires, you may *want* a plan to become debt free or to save more money.

These goals are pleasant and fulfilling ones. Often, our lives can take a detour on the road to happiness, and women find themselves facing other unanticipated needs and desires. I often hear my women clients define other concerns and goals for themselves: "What happens to my security and insurance if my husband divorces me?" "What will happen with my husband's retirement if we should divorce?" "What happens to the grocery money I've saved over the past ten years to put toward our retirement planning; am I going to get anything out of it if we are no longer married?"

Prenuptial Agreements

First and foremost, women who are anticipating marriage or whose marriage may be strained, need to understand their state laws governing divorce, separate property, community property, and custody issues. In some states such as Texas, a community property state, property acquired during the course of marriage is usually owned equally by husband and wife regardless of title. You should check with an attorney to determine your situation.

In America today, more and more women, who are entering second or third marriages, are taking a careful look at these issues. As one client told me, "Mary, it's not a matter of believing or not believing in 'till death do us part. If I didn't believe in the institution and the possibility of a happy marriage, I wouldn't be pursuing it again. Being single is socially acceptable in our society today, but I *want* to marry. My focus on financial safeguards has more to do with being accountable for my own actions. When you are in love and enraptured with the hope and possibility of a brighter future with someone you think you want to share your life with, you believe in the fairy tale and look at the world with rose colored glasses to such an extent that you do not protect yourself. I can see young women in their early years out of college getting married with stars in their eyes. Most of these young women have little to lose this early in life. A prenuptial agreement becomes imperative in a second or third marriage when women and men both have financial responsibilities for their own children. A prenuptial alone can't protect against all financial issues in the future, or from being 100 percent accountable for the joint debt that my new husband and I create together, but it can keep me from losing what little I have saved up to this point in time. Some women think of a prenuptial agreement as an admission of a belief that their marriage will not last. To me it seems smarter to have one and enjoy every anniversary year as a celebration that it wasn't necessary, rather than be in divorce court calling yourself naïve for dismissing the idea when you were in love and not thinking straight."

Not all generations of women with whom I deal have such strong feelings. I've witnessed more women reconsidering the way they approach a second marriage. It seems that more new women clients come to me every year who have created prenuptial agreements and consider them to be "financial insurance of another kind." As one woman who is also an attorney explained, "This issue gets at the core of trust between a couple. If the future husband and wife cannot discuss matters as emotional and sensitive as an agreement of this kind, it probably means that they have not yet developed an ability to communicate with each other about serious real life issues. Such honest communication is imperative if the marriage is to last. Therefore, if the discussion about the prenuptial agreement doesn't get off on the right foot, it most likely indicates other serious flaws in the relationship. Most women have success with an agreement if a lawyer discusses the pros and cons with the couple together. The lawyer, as a neutral third party, can position the benefits of the agreements for both parties. This keeps the discussion on a nonconfrontational basis. When it's all over, couples seem to welcome the experience, because it reveals the deep-seated feelings of their future partner."

Defining Your Wants, Needs and Desires

After you've finally selected your financial professional of choice and you're preparing for that first appointment to discuss your needs for the future, it is necessary for you to have your personal goals and objectives clearly identified and stated before that appointment. Here are qualitative questions that will help you define your own wants, needs and desires for the future:

- ◆ If you've already accumulated a sizeable estate, have you made provisions to protect your assets from exposure to lawsuits, estate taxes, or inheritance taxes?
- ◆ If your spouse is a successful business owner, are you confident that your personal interests are protected in the event of his or her death, disability, or financial disaster?
- ◆ If your spouse is a successful business owner and should die, are you confident that you understand what happens to the ownership of the business and what effect that selling the business has on your daily lifestyle?
- ◆ What type of job or career do you envision for yourself in five years?

- Do you see yourself owning or starting your own business some day? Do you think you will do this on your own or with a partner?
- Are you a successful business owner and considering a succession plan?
- If you are a business owner, does your employee benefit package need to be reviewed?
- If you are a business owner, do you feel that you may need to review and talk about some business strategies?
- Do you have any future educational goals for yourself or for members of your family?
- If you are responsible for the care of children, do you plan to remain at home or must you work to earn an income?
- Describe the type of education and schools you envision your children or grandchildren attending.
- Have you had thoughts of divorce?
- To what extent can genetic health issues impact your future?
- Is there a church, community, or art organization in which you are a dedicated and active member?
- Do you have an ideal place where you want to "settle down" or do you prefer to remain free to travel and relocate easily?
- Is it important for you to own your own home or condo? Is a vacation home or second residence in your plans?
- If you choose to raise a family, will you want to buy a larger home?
- After your children are raised and no longer living at home, will you plan to move into a smaller home?
- How old will you be when you retire? Where would you like to live? And what type of lifestyle will you require?
- Will you be financially responsible or personally involved in caring for special needs children, grandchildren, or aging parents in the future? Are you familiar with the decisions that need to be made when selecting an appropriate care facility?
- Do you plan to inherit any additional income, real estate or other holdings?
- What habits in life as you are living it right now would you be willing to "give up," if necessary, to attain your long-term goals?

These are critical and emotional questions whose answers carry lifestyle implications. If your attorney, CPA and financial professional are to help you achieve the goals you've established in your life, you must consider life to be a step-by-step journey. Financial success and well-being can not be accomplished in a day—not even by winning the lottery. You must realize that achieving any goals generally requires a program that coordinates legal and tax issues, insurance, savings, and investments. No one aspect will accomplish it for you.

I believe the process of soul searching and defining personal goals for your life should be as important as the outcome itself. Thinking about your trials, blessings, dreams, and goals is an affirmation of your being. These help define what you have been and what you have learned during the years you have been surrounded by the beauty of the world we have been given to play and work in.

These questions help you rekindle the motivation and commitment to achieve the milestones you have and will continue to set for yourself. While you do this, I encourage you to give yourself the luxury of quiet time to do your thinking. Perhaps it's a walk in the woods or along a stream while picking berries. Perhaps it's time musing at a window with the aroma of potpourri and tea or mulled cider steaming around you. Perhaps it's a long walk along the beach, alone and at peace. The time you spend in reviewing your life and setting new goals will be cherished for many years because it signifies again that you are assuming responsibility and control of your future. Determining your wants, needs and desires is another step along this financial journey of your life.

When it comes time for the appointment with your financial professional, you should have spent a great deal of time soul searching about the wishes and dreams of your life. Any future planning must consider the ups and downs possible in life if you are to gain confidence about your well-being and financial success in the future.

—— *Melva* ——

Melva always knew her wants and desires, but it took her a long time to achieve them. Early in 1993, she came to visit me at the recommendation of her attorney. She was a petite grandmother with ash grey hair, cut short and tapered at the back. She had recently been widowed and felt a sincere need to get life insurance so that she could leave an inheritance for her children.

Our conversation revealed that she had a firm resolve for saving and that she and her husband had been focused on saving. She was in her mid-sixties and healthy. As a result, Melva estimated that the insurance proceeds that she received following her husband's death would all be required to support her for the rest of her life. She talked about what a wonderful husband he had been and how much she truly missed his sparkle and their happy times together. She commended him for leaving her financially secure. However, because she was in excellent health, she had concerns about how far the amount would go if she was fortunate to live a long life.

In a tone of quiet reserve, Melva explained that her husband never felt she needed insurance. He believed that insurance was for the man as the head of the household, not for the woman. She said that he never understood her feelings or her desires when she realized that the amount of insurance he had for her would be needed to sustain her through life, but that she would not be able to leave an inheritance to their children and grandchildren when she died.

She anticipated entering a nursing home someday and knew that the nursing home might eventually assume the legal ownership of her home and real estate as payment for her residency. Therefore, she did not want to base her children's inheritance on the asset of her home when it could be reassigned to a nursing home before she died. She was concerned as she relayed a story to me about two of her friends. She explained that these women signed over their homes and moved to a nursing home only to "outlive" their arrangement. After eighteen months, her friends were facing the end of the contracted agreement with the nursing home—alive with no place to call home, and nowhere to go.

Melva related to me that she had been a traditional home-maker all her life and did not work outside of the home as is customary for "this newer generation." She was with her children and grandchildren every day; they were "her life." Melva explained that she had two wonderful children—a married daughter and a son who was divorced and raising a ten-year-old son. She felt comfortable with her daughter's future because her daughter's life seemed to be financially secure. She had genuine concerns for her son who was a single parent challenged to provide all the financial and emotional necessities for a growing child. As Melva described all the details of their lives, her gentleness and caring were apparent. Indeed, her children truly were the center of her world now that her husband had died.

Because Melva was not involved with the family's financial affairs while her husband was alive, she exuded a zeal to learn everything about insurance—something she had wanted a great deal but something that was denied to her. She vigorously asked questions and wanted to see proposals. She wanted to review, understand and analyze every option. I gave her an envelope of materials to study, and I can say that I cannot remember seeing anyone ever so excited about reviewing mounds of gray and unappealing paperwork as Melva—like a child in a candy store.

During her learning process, Melva was solicited for insurance by a direct mail company. Because direct mail companies do not carry the expenses associated with maintaining local offices to service policyholders or expenses associated with payments to financial professionals, the cash values in this company's policy were higher in the early years. Ultimately, however, price was not a determining factor in Melva's choice. She was focused on the values of her policy at her death, and she was focused on service. She chose to work with a financial professional because of the value-added service and because she could ask questions and learn. She wanted me to be present at her funeral to be the financial strength for her family when she was gone.

At age sixty-seven, Melva's excellent health and vitality made it possible for her to obtain insurance affordably after a favorable medical exam. She felt an incredible sense of accomplishment to be able to provide this for her children. The excitement she felt about having her own insurance was unbelievable—even to me. Melva affirmed, "I have wanted this for a very long time as a testimony to my own personal worth as a woman and the love I have for my children. It enables me to financially give them much more after I'm gone than what I am able give them while I am alive."

By saving with her husband during his lifetime, Melva secured an income to satisfy her basic needs after he died. Her obtaining coverage on her own, at age sixty-seven, satisfied her desires to leave a substantial financial legacy to her children.

STEP 6
Assessing Your Present Financial Health

Telling All

When you and your financial professional meet to begin your planning, you should be ready to tell all. Many women feel uncomfortable providing financial data. Some even consider it to be an invasion of privacy. But for your financial professional to complete a fact find that can thoroughly address your wants, needs, and desires, you must be prepared to tell all in this beginning stage of your planning interview.

I suggest you consider a thorough *fact find* as a critical and indispensable next step. (In the financial services industry, the terms *fact find* and *fact-finding interview* are used to describe a process by which your assets, income, expenses, and other family information are recorded, analyzed, and reviewed relative to your short-term and long-term goals.) It is necessary for a *diagnosis* of your present financial condition and must precede any recommendations for future planning.

There are many analogies found in the world of the other professionals with whom you work. For instance, a CPA needs information about your earning and spending patterns to complete your tax documents. Your physician attempts to know all of your family's medical background as well as your own symptoms before prescribing a procedure or remedy. When creating a will, an attorney needs to know whom you want to care for your children in the event of your death. Similarly, the financial professional needs information in order to provide for your financial welfare.

Because insurance is not an immediate or tangible product, its benefits often are misunderstood. Insurance is not only a benefit you can draw on in the long term, but it can also play a part in your overall lifestyle and goals. A professional should ask many questions about your monthly income and expenses. You should also be willing to provide family and employer data. Also, be leery if you are not asked extensive questions to provide this data. I cannot say enough about working with someone who is thorough in finding out the financial facts about your life.

If you are considering the purchase of securities, the SEC/NASD require that a registered representative ask "suitability" questions under the NASD Rules of Fair Practice, rule 2310, "Know Your Customers." Ultimately, for your benefit and protection, make sure that the financial professional you choose to work with conducts a thorough fact find to obtain background information about your financial condition.

Building Blocks of a Financial Portfolio

It all starts with writing down your dreams. Many of my women clients compare completion of the fact find to building a house. For the house, you need an architectural plan, a foundation, lumber, brick, mortar, water, heat, electricity, and so on. You need to have all the components together to create a home that is strong, beautiful, and satisfies your dreams. Similarly, a strong financial program that can accomplish your goals will include prenuptial agreements, wills, living wills, and trusts in addition to business agreements. Some if not all of these financial elements will also be included:

- ♦ Property and casualty insurance to help protect your home, possessions, and vehicle as assets and to help protect against unforeseen liabilities that may result from accidents or claims against you.
- ♦ Suitable individual disability income protection in the event that you can no longer provide monthly income for household needs.
- ♦ Business overhead expense coverage payable to your company to help cover monthly expenses such as rent, utilities, and employee salaries if you are a business owner who becomes disabled as described in the policy.
- ♦ Group life insurance as well as individual term or cash value life insurance proceeds can be used to help fund expenses of

burial, food, clothing and housing for the remaining family members.

♦ Life insurance to fund a trust.

♦ Life insurance to help pay estate taxes.

♦ Tax deferred products such as life insurance and annuities.

♦ Liquid savings vehicles such as certificates of deposits and money market accounts.

♦ Securities such as mutual funds, stocks, bonds, variable life insurance, and variable annuities.

Caveat emptor! Let the buyer beware. Purchasing life insurance and sophisticated investment products is a paper-intensive and detail-oriented process. There should be an extensive amount of time spent on gathering information about you. Be wary of writing any checks or signing on the dotted line within an hour of meeting any new financial professional. Be proactive during the fact finding process and ask many questions. I cannot over emphasize to women, that in the midst of this data gathering session, if you are uncomfortable and seem to be the target of aggressive tactics or pressured sales—the financial professional you are working with is probably not right for you.

Information to Provide

Many companies and financial professionals have created their own written questionnaires to gather data as part of their fact-finding process. (A sample questionnaire is included in: *American Dream Women: A Workbook & Planning Guide.*) Overall, any questionnaire will inquire about all necessary aspects of your finances. Be certain to provide:

♦ Auto, homeowners or renters, disability income, and/or life insurance policies.

♦ The last two year's federal income tax statements.

♦ All interest or dividend earnings and account balance statements from: certificates of deposit, bank savings accounts, money market accounts, mutual funds, stocks, bonds, securities, annuities, 401(k), 403(b), or any other pension plans you may have started.

- ◆ Handbook of benefits from your employer and any employee benefit statements.
- ◆ All of the above information that relates to any business interest.
- ◆ A detailed description of your monthly house and utility expenses, car loans and maintenance costs, credit card balances, home equity or other loans, medical bills, grocery receipts, entertainment expenses, average checking account activity on a monthly basis.
- ◆ Information about any legal wills or trust documents.
- ◆ Any other information that relates to what you have done in the past to provide for your financial future.

The financial professional will review this information and make recommendations based on your wants, needs, and desires. This gathering of your personal data is a way of cleaning house and getting all of your information—formal papers or informal notes—in order and in one place. (*American Dream Women: A Workbook & Planning Guide* offers an organized process to help assist you in this challenge.) Often, we go through life assuming that all of our affairs are in order only to find out in an emergency that they are not.

At this point, I'd like to address women business owners. Even more so than individuals, the business owner must plan to review and amend the fact-find data annually. You will see many changes that have taken place since the inception of your business. Changes in your employee benefit structure may cause you to consider profit sharing. Raising the deductibles on the employee health insurance plan could lower premiums and make dollars available to spend in other areas. Maybe it is time to consider a disability income protection program for your employees, or there may be a need for life insurance on key employees.

At times, a company will send you letters regarding updated information about your policy or other products you own (health insurance, disability income insurance, life insurance, mutual funds, annuities, stocks, bonds, certificates of deposit). The law requires that any significant changes affecting products or values be communicated in writing and mailed to the policyholder or owner directly from the company that issued the product. You should take care that this correspondence be filed with your important papers. Then you should demand that the financial professional or registered representative explain the changes to you and the impact of these changes on the rest of your financial program as well.

Life changes, and as a result, whether you are single, married with children, a single parent, or a woman business owner, the review and assessment of your financial program relative to the current interest rate environment, your current lifestyle and expenses, and your business needs is a process that never really ends. You owe it to yourself to review these financial affairs annually. Consider updates to your planning more important than updating your wardrobe. When this cycle repeats in your life, you know you are well underway to staying on top of it all—*you are* in control of your financial affairs.

STEP 7
Determining What You Can Afford

── Theresa ──

Theresa came to interview me in early spring of 1985. She was a tall, gorgeous blonde. She was vivacious, with the smile and enthusiasm of a twenty-one-year-old student, although she had turned forty the previous November. Her poise made people watch her across a room; she commanded a second look. It was hard to believe that she was the mother of three college-age children. She wore a designer outfit, finely tailored of silk and linen with sandals of fabric and texture to match. Her 24-carat jewelry sparkled. Even her rouge and lipstick complemented the hues of her wardrobe. You couldn't help notice that her manicure and pedicure were fresh, and her accessories were carefully chosen as well. By the end of our first visit, it was apparent that everything in Theresa's life—her outings, her vacations, her parties, her clothes—was designed with great care, except her financial future.

Theresa was adamant about change. She explained that she was born and raised "in serenity" on a peaceful farm in the Tennessee horse country. Her tasks included early morning visits to the chicken coop to collect eggs for breakfast, while her younger brothers picked garden vegetables for the day's meals. The family farm provided an ample supply of meat from steers, pigs, and poultry. There was an ebullient pride in her story about how she had grown to accumulate a taste for knowledge about the finer things in life long after her humble beginnings.

She took special pride in explaining that, when she was a young girl, she learned to sew and tailor dresses from gingham and checkered pattern sacks that were a bonus for purchase of a hundred pounds of flour. She felt special because the material was cut, washed, and creatively sewn "just for her" by her Mom. This was a real treat since she was from a family of ten children.

The work ethic that was ingrained for Theresa's family became evident as she recalled the strength of her father, Jack, and her mother, Gayle. Her dad was also one of ten children. He worked his way through college in Chattanooga by playing drums in a jazz band. Jack was determined to be successful and dreamed of having a chain of filling stations. America was taking to the new post-World War II freedom of the highway. Jack and Gayle saved and worked very hard on the farm until they had enough to lease their first filling station. His enterprise grew to a $1.7 million chain.

Gayle was a city girl from a prestigious family in Atlanta. Bred in high style and accustomed to gourmet butler service at every meal, she attended the famous Ward Belmont finishing school in Nashville and excelled as a ballerina. She was always picture perfect in her appearance—complete with hat and gloves for church.

In the 1930s, '40s, and '50s, a woman's "place" truly was at home. Gayle was adamant that the more time and nurturing given to children, the better adjusted, well mannered and responsible they would be as adults. With a full-time mother working at home, the children were trained to make their beds every morning, keep a perfectly clean and orderly room, do homework before supper, and enjoy friends and entertainment only after a rigorous regimen of household chores and family responsibilities. With a large family, Theresa's mother had her hands full with cooking, canning, cleaning, sewing and raising the little ones. The family was active in church and had a family pew in the front row where strict silence, behavior, and manners were required. The family was devout, religious, and prayed together daily while kneeling at the couch in thanksgiving for good health and blessings received. Their social life consisted of involvement in their rural community—pie socials, rummage sales, and church picnics. They generously gave to the community, and in addition to raising their children, they sponsored the education of seven young men through the seminary.

As husband and wife, Jack and Gayle felt that a woman's role was to be centered in the home and not involved with finances.

These were not the days of dual incomes or dual income expectations; therefore, family finances were the husband's role. Mother's job was teacher and homemaker responsible for nurturing a family with social manners and solid morals. Jack gave Gayle a monthly allowance to cover grocery and household expenses. These were times of cash spending only. Nothing was bought unless it was bought with cash. Children were not privy to the financial affairs of the family, which Theresa later learned was critical behavior if a family today is to grow and live within its means.

As her story turned to her own family, Theresa's financial stress was revealed as she explained her early days after marrying Glenn, her high school sweetheart, in 1958. They both, along with her brothers, were molded by her father to someday run the family business. Theresa's goal was to learn the family business and enjoy home life and raising children. She never expected that her income would be necessary to support the family while Glenn's income was needed to put back into the family business.

Her father died, and the family watched the business quickly crumble because there was no life insurance that could have been used to help stabilize the business. Tears filled Theresa's eyes when she recalled that the funeral procession for her father was three miles long in tribute to this very well respected, gentle, and giving man. Theresa, Glenn, and her brothers involved in the business were not knowledgeable, nor did they have ample funds to keep the business going. Without money to cover the cash flow, the business soon died.

With Theresa's and Glenn's goals and livelihood in jeopardy, they both sought other jobs. After six years of marriage, she had three children of her own and was raising her younger brothers and sisters because of her mother's illness and institutionalization. Theresa found herself in a dual-income world she had never experienced at home. She became resentful of trying to find ways to keep it all together, juggling a full-time job, sewing clothes for the children, having healthy meals on the table every evening, cleaning, doing laundry, being active in church, doing gardening and cutting grass. She was overwhelmed.

Their dual incomes also created expectations and demands for personal rewards for the sacrifices which were being made by both Theresa and Glenn. They wanted the luxuries of purchasing nicer clothes, dinner, and dancing. Things were starting to accumulate. Buying on credit with charge cards became a lifestyle. Both she and Glenn wanted new cars, furniture, carpeting, and vacations badly enough to undergo extreme financial stress to have them. Their friends created a peer pressure for accumulating things.

Theresa laughed as she described the typical family meals back then as they struggled to pay for the trappings of the household. Dinners were: pressure cooker Swiss steak or fried chicken with potatoes on Sunday, chicken and turkey pot pies with fruit cocktail throughout the week, grilled cheese and tomato soup on Thursday, macaroni and cheese with fish sticks on Friday, and jiffy steaks or beans and franks as a special treat on Saturday. The family couldn't wait for summer when they could have a cookout with hot dogs on the grill.

At that point in her life, Theresa's definition of wealth was to immediately have all the things that her mother took thirty years to struggle for; she "wanted it now" and "would pay for it over time." Whereas her parents didn't purchase anything unless they had cash, Theresa and Glenn began what she called "a period of debt addiction." They created an endless cycle of credit card buying and the payment stress that goes with it. The cycle of credit card buying and binge spending as a reward for hard work continued for Theresa and Glenn for more than twenty years.

It took Theresa twenty years to realize that as long as their life was dominated by debt addiction there could be no accumulation of wealth. She recalled "fear at forty" and explained, "Suddenly the lights went on. Things and stuff began losing their value while retirement concerns were becoming serious emotional issues looming for both of us." Together, Theresa and Glenn were committed to a lifestyle change in order to aggressively accumulate wealth over the next twenty-five years. They relocated to make a fresh start. They had used all their previous savings for the move and to sustain them for one year while their new careers were being established. When Glenn relocated, he lost his benefits and insurance.

Even though they were unemployed when they relocated, their long-term dream was to have a $2 million nest egg for retirement. They both chose commission jobs for the income potential: Glenn started in real estate; Theresa worked with cosmetics. When Theresa came to see me, she was determined. After a fact find to assess their financial condition, she began to put into action long-term goals so that some day she could go back to the uncomplicated serene life she remembered on the farm as a child.

She committed to put money away into her savings account with an obligation of no less than 10 percent of their combined gross income. She totaled their monthly credit card expenses and committed to paying double payments for three years until all were paid. As a couple, they committed to refrain from purchasing anything unnecessary and started to follow a strict budget. Glenn was to receive a modest inheritance to be paid over ten years as certificates of deposit became due. We created a program to put these deposits into mutual funds and diversify the money into three funds.

Theresa and Glenn made strict commitments to each other that money had to be put away for savings first. Each month they would write a check for savings "as if it were a bill" in order to "pay themselves first" as she called it. When the credit card debt was gone after the three years, they took the money that was being used to pay off the debt and applied it to their long-term wealth accumulation program. They also purchased a properly designed disability income and life insurance program that would meet their needs. They took any bonuses and salary increases and put them into a liquid savings account so when premiums came due, they had the money to pay. Theresa quipped, "We went back to the early days of macaroni and cheese with fish sticks and started to laugh about how life had changed at forty. Instead of chicken pot pies to buy furniture and carpeting and stuff, we were eating macaroni and cheese so we could aggressively save."

On one of Theresa's subsequent visits, she told me that she and Glenn had just purchased a dream house on a peaceful and serene fishing lake in the North Woods where they were planning to retire after they left the city. I knew how disciplined her savings had become, and I was amazed that she could still be able to purchase prime real estate. I asked her, "How did you ever manage that?"

She winked, "Macaroni and cheese with fish sticks."

Know What You Can Afford

After the financial professional leaves the fact-finding interview with financial information to review, most women become concerned about their ability to pay for the recommendations that will come next. Hopefully, the days are past when agents took a quick look at your policies, told you what to buy, and you could not afford it over the long term.

You have done your homework. You've proceeded through your interviewing process. You've chosen your financial professional. You've gathered all your financial information and turned it over for review.

All recommendations for insurance or investment plans must be understood in terms of your goals as well as your ability to save over the long term. Buying financial products is not like buying a winter wardrobe that would be forgotten or replaced next year. For a financial program to succeed over time, payments must be sustained over the long term. You must comfortably be able to afford payments.

Theresa and Glenn learned the process of wealth accumulation the hard way, but after twenty years, they realized that being *"wealthy" does not mean accumulating material "things" that symbolize a perception of what it means to be wealthy*. Accumulating wealth means accumulating savings over time. This is done by protecting your earning power to sustain cash flow into savings, insurance, and investments and by guarding against spending that drains cash flow.

A fundamental step in any financial strategy for the future is understanding your monthly overhead and living expenses. What women want in life is often a relentless driving force; yet they don't realize what they must do financially to accomplish their goals, or what short-term tradeoffs and sacrifices they must make to achieve financial success over the long term. Any professional to whom you are entrusting your planning cannot recommend a realistic program for you without knowledge of your income, all of your expenses and cash flow in relationship to what you need and want.

The Generation of Entitlement and Debt Addiction

To achieve their dreams, many women have asked me, "Why must I be debt free? What will I have to do to become debt free? Will you help me with a budget?"

There are more college educated adults and couples in America today than ever. The sacrifices and time spent in attaining a technical, professional, trade and academic education in a post-war economy have created an attitude of entitlement for the Baby Boomers and their children alike. The information age and the ease of advertising in a global marketplace have brought the allure of goods and services from around the world into our televisions at home and into our shopping malls. Time spent shopping at the mall constitutes a major pastime for American consumers. Our affluent society believes it must have the status of material wealth as a reward for arduous work or education. Status symbols such as luxury cars, designer clothing, jewelry, and fabulous vacations are all easily purchased at the mall, by phone, or on line with credit cards.

The ease of obtaining credit in our country has desensitized consumers to the long-term consequences of buy-now-pay-later spending. College coeds get credit cards; it's a sign that "they've arrived" into the adult world. She carries her department store cards; he carries his as well. When young couples marry today, they are eager for the revenue of two incomes, yet have seemed to lose focus that they both have brought a healthy stream of debt into their new marriage. Likewise, many couples are adamant about purchasing a home before they are married. They tell me, "After all—we've studied and worked hard, and we deserve it." What they don't realize is that they *do not deserve* the yoke of indebtedness that will sometimes prevent them from accumulating real wealth and saving for retirement until much too late. A large number of younger Americans, especially young married couples, live lifestyles beyond their means. They do it with the help of credit cards. Because they can afford the monthly credit card payments as a result of acquiring consumer goods, their credit card spending creates an illusion that they have material wealth. But they do not understand the short- and long-term costs of accumulating such debt. *There can be no long-term accumulation of future wealth if a couple carries debt that prevents them from saving 10-20 percent of their gross income.* This is true if the balance of a couples' disposable income after food, clothing, housing, and transportation, is used to pay credit card debt rather than saved to earn additional accumulation.

Debt Reduction

If a client carries a heavy load of debt, my focus as a financial professional is to take time to understand the debt situation. My advice is always to make *removing debt the first priority*. This is accomplished as follows:

♦ A two- or three-year period is set aside with debt reduction as the priority before any disposable income is used for cash spending.

♦ Clients must agree not to make purchases unless they have the cash in hand. Buying habits that include purchasing with deferred payments are not an option to becoming debt free. To believe a repetitive cycle of credit card debt will not hinder wealth accumulation is erroneous.

♦ Accelerated or double payments to pay off credit cards and/or consolidating them into an equity loan may be necessary.

The purpose of any financial program is to accomplish goals within a framework of consistently and methodically saving money. There are other reasons to make debt reduction a priority:

♦ It creates disciplined spending habits. It creates a new mindset based only on cash purchases. If focus is to eliminate $10,000 to $20,000 of credit card debt, it will be less likely to create new debt given the sacrifices that must be made to double payments.

♦ Concentration to pay off debt creates disciplined saving habits. Once the debt is paid, the $500 to $800 monthly payment should be instantly available cash flow for investment. Gratification becomes swift and wonderful when this cycle begins.

The Cost of Waiting

When women begin careers in their early twenties and become more stable in their thirties, they enter what I call a "spending and debt cycle" as they acquire homes, expensive possessions, marry, and build families. It's usually not until age forty that the fear of debt addiction or lost time becomes strong enough to force a change in attitude, lifestyle, buying habits and spending habits. For many women with whom I work, a realization about the cost of waiting is enough to catapult them into new savings habits with great zeal.

One client needed to remove debt. At age forty-two, she was depressed to realize that since college she had progressed in her career with six different jobs, had moved ten times and had earned more than $450,000. Yet she had accumulated no "real" savings to speak of and carried $25,000 in debt. As she viewed it, she "had nothing to show for twenty years in her career." She summed up her change in attitude this way: "I started to picture savings in terms of the long-term value of some of my excesses in spending. I used to love to buy new shoes—and only the best shoes. It wasn't difficult for me to spend $200 for a pair of designer shoes every month. I considered it a reward for my high stress job. When I realized that if I bought less expensive shoes and saved $200 each month over the 20 years since I've been out of college, today that 'shoe money' would be worth more than $130,000. How many pairs of shoes does a woman really need anyway!"

Clients' credit card payment habits and spending habits have proven that very little wealth accumulation can occur in an aggressive savings approach if the majority of their income feeds a frenzied cycle of paying off old credit card debt and creating new credit card debt. Also, clients have demonstrated that modest regular savings will accumulate if any discipline to save can be achieved. One couple in their twenties was staggered to realize that by limiting eating out to once a week, and going out to the clubs twice a month rather than twice a week, they could save $100 a month.

How to Allocate Your Money

Once you've satisfied your debt and attained the discipline of regular savings, you can determine what you can afford. It is necessary to understand the relationship between your checking account, short-term savings account, and future finances.

Imagine three circles or three reservoirs of money. The first is your checking account; the second is your short-term savings account; the third is for future accumulation.

Future financial strategies need to link these principles, and your financial focus on each of them should never waver. (See diagram below.) Keeping in mind the relationship among these areas can help you maintain consciousness of your net income and expenses, help ensure that you have a short-term savings in place to protect for unforeseen events, and that the first two reservoirs be full before you begin a disciplined, long-term savings program. If you are always being forced to borrow from what you consider a long-term savings account, then it canot grow or accumulate based on your goals.

Based on the fact find and the expense analysis you completed earlier, by analyzing your *checking account*, you should

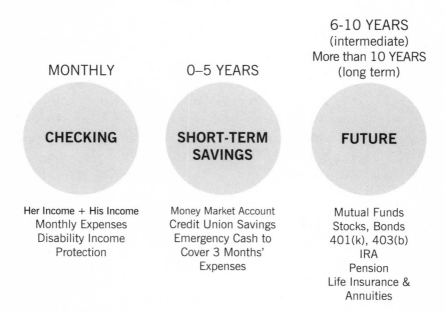

MONTHLY	0–5 YEARS	6-10 YEARS (intermediate) More than 10 YEARS (long term)
CHECKING	**SHORT-TERM SAVINGS**	**FUTURE**
Her Income + His Income Monthly Expenses Disability Income Protection	Money Market Account Credit Union Savings Emergency Cash to Cover 3 Months' Expenses	Mutual Funds Stocks, Bonds 401(k), 403(b) IRA Pension Life Insurance & Annuities

know the relationship of your expenses to your income, and what, if any, excess dollars are available. Your checking account ideally reflects one month's income and expenses. There are many young couples who have a checking account balance large enough to cover a year's worth of expenses. I do not recommend this because it is more difficult to remain focused on the three distinct budgets you have created for monthly expenses, short-term savings and future investments.

The *short-term savings* circle is a short-term fund for liquid cash in an emergency—in case your furnace breaks, or your car needs major repair. This amount is typically enough to cover one to six months' expenses; a minimum of three month's expenses is a good rule of thumb. This reserve of money should be accumulated for several reasons. Not only is it available as a cushion in the event that you become disabled (in the interim before you receive any disability income payments), but also it creates a kind of mental security blanket. I strongly recommend this fund for my clients. The feeling of confidence of having it can help provide strong self-esteem and help eliminate some of the worry resulting from an emergency or other binge spending that has diminished your long-term savings. I have found that a client who wants to eliminate this short-term savings fund generally has more difficulty living on a budget and maintaining regular and disciplined payments into a long-term savings vehicle because of "fear" of not having liquid cash available.

Savings vehicles for this type of short-term savings reserve may be a credit union, a bank savings account, or a money market account through a securities firm. Whatever vehicle you select, it should always be a reserve to satisfy short-term liquid cash needs rather than a reserve for long-term investment.

The *future accumulation* reservoir is considered for a longer period of time. You are seeking long-term accumulation of cash in this reservoir. This typically includes any 401(k), 403(b), other pension or profit sharing plans and annuities, which are long-term financial products designed for retirement purposes. Withdrawals are subject to normal income tax treatment and early withdrawals may be subject to surrender charges. Early withdrawals may also be subject to a federal income tax penalty, depending on your age when you make the withdrawal. Cash value life insurance could also be included as an asset in this category. If the purpose is to provide an income to your family after you die, a rule of thumb is that you begin an insurance portfolio based on eight to fifteen times your annual income. The amount varies on a number of factors, including the amount of insurance you qualify to obtain.

After you've eliminated your debt, have built a short-term emergency fund, and have begun saving in your future accumulation reservoir, the fun begins. During the process, your banker, CPA, or financial professional can help you calculate the nest egg you would like to accumulate for retirement and help you determine how much you should contribute on a monthly or annual basis to achieve it. All professionals involved in the financial services industry have compound interest tables that can illustrate the growth potential of your savings over time based on various interest rates to help you understand potential returns.

Everyone wants to save more money. One question I hear is how do I know the best way to save? How does a CD or certificate of deposit work? What will a money market do for me? What do mutual funds do? How does insurance work?

Saving more money can be accomplished in many different ways. You can save money on a *non-qualified basis* as well as a *qualified basis*. [*Qualified* generally refers to an IRA or similar retirement plan created by an employer for the benefit of eligible employees, such as a pension, profit sharing, 401(k), 403(b)]. You generally cannot consider these funds to be liquid, which means that you cannot access them easily until retirement; any withdrawal before you reach a government-specified age may incur substantial IRS penalties along with current income. Perhaps as you save your money, you want to have access to it quickly, that is you want it to be liquid and available to you in case of emergency. Vehicles that can accomplish this are money market accounts, savings accounts, mutual funds, and (with some limitations) cash value life insurance.

For a thorough understanding of these concepts relative to your personal circumstances, you must discuss these concepts with your CPA, banker, or financial professional. Ultimately, the choice of products you choose must be yours—not theirs—based on what is suitable for your situation, your overall availability of funds, and your needs.

The investment marketplace is dynamic, and interest rates are always changing. That is why it is imperative for you to monitor values quarterly or annually to assess how your investments have gone up or down relative your previous projections and dreams. It's important that you realize that financial professionals cannot make investments on your behalf. *That is why it is your responsibility to require that your professional team continues to keep you aware of the marketplace and to determine if your portfolio is positioned for the highest potential of earnings based on your long-term objectives and risk tolerance.*

After understanding the relationships among your monthly checking account, short-term savings account and future investment account, the next lesson in planning for your financial future is to learn how each relates to any employee benefits you may have.

STEP 8
Understanding Your Company Benefits

—— *Maria* ——

Maria was a young woman from an uneducated working family; her mother and father expressed the work ethic with a stoic pride in their home, children, and jobs. To follow her dream meant that Maria worked her way through college washing dishes in a restaurant. Her grade point average was always at or near perfect. She was a petite brunette. Maria was not a beauty, but her warm heart, poise, and grace made people remember her—as well as her unusual hands that were large from years of masonry, roofing, and carpentry work with her father. She was petite, not because she was diminutive, but because she was short. Maria was determined to work her way out of the old, dirty, blue collar industrial town where she was born and raised. She graduated summa cum laude from a prestigious college, received a scholarship to graduate school, married, and divorced early.

Since becoming my client, Maria had told me many times that her goal in those early years of her life and career was to achieve a superior education and a white collar job. She was a classic over achiever. Her creativity blossomed with her musical talent and writing ability. Nothing impaired her focus; for she believed strongly that if she was going to compete in a man's world, she needed to be well educated. She believed that women needed to have three times more education than men to earn respect in the American workplace. After several years working in corporations, her intuition seemed to be justified. At that time, Maria witnessed a working world where women having more credentials and experience in white collar corporate jobs earned less than men for doing the same work. That harsh reality fueled the fire of her drive and ambition "to be the best." Over the next few years, she went to night school and received a second master's degree in business management. Years of full-time work and night school continued until she had also earned the national board accreditation that she coveted so highly. In all, she brought twenty-four years of education to her career accompanied by more than twenty years of full-time experience.

As she told me when she became my client, Maria was thirty-three when she had remarried—this time to an older man with children, ages nine, ten and thirteen. His financial obligations to them in their formative years and impending college years meant that she was responsible for a major portion of their living expenses and those of her own children she hoped to have someday. This did not bother her because she was in love with someone who seemed to be more mature and stable—financially, it would all work out with time when his children were grown.

Three months after being married privately in judge's chambers, Maria's hopes for a new future and family of her own came to a halt. One night she had a dream of a serious illness. Her intuition had been right many times previously—enough to prompt her to seek medical testing. Within the week, medical examinations confirmed she had uterine cancer.

A life that had been focused on education and a career took the back seat to obtaining second medical opinions and checking with her employer about the types of medical benefits and disability benefits she would have. She learned that short-term salary continuation benefits for several weeks after surgery were provided for ninety days. But if she elected to consider additional postoperative procedures her finances would not be secure. The cost for the chemotherapy and radiology procedures would be covered, but if she grew ill and couldn't work in the following weeks, which was a certainty with such medical treatment, she would not be on full salary, and there would be some money *but not enough* money to pay the bills at home as well as help her husband with the financial needs of his three growing children.

In those bitter next few weeks, Maria also learned that in her state's legal system, Maria's good job and income actually made it possible for the birth mother of the children to request additional income from the children's father; his marriage to Maria increased his "ability to pay" to his ex-wife. Maria was disillusioned to learn that her sacrifices were empowering for another woman—and detrimental to her own financial condition at that time. According to the law, the father's obligations to his children came first before any obligations to his home or second wife.

Maria elected to have surgery. Her financial situation caused her to return to work after the three-month short-term disability period ended. She refused the traditional therapies of Western medicine, and through reading and research, she embraced homeopathic remedies. The small town where she lived had no contact with such alternative medicine or doctors. Her physician insisted that full recovery was doubtful and pressured her to begin chemotherapy and radiation treatments.

For the first time since she began her journey on the fast track in high school, she felt vulnerable and alone. All of her education, career, and dreams could not buy her health. She faced her hospital stay knowing she had no financial help from her second husband. To make matters emotionally worse, the hospital placed her in the maternity ward that intensified her anxiety at not being able to have children of her own. How had her life derailed to such an extent?

In our talks about those days, Maria could not stress enough how she wished that she had taken the time to understand the benefits of the plan she had at work. The details didn't seem to matter—until she learned she had cancer; then it was just too late.

Maria was hard on herself; she had felt "mortally naïve" as she called it. She trusted too many other people, financial professionals as well as her husband, to guide her when she did not totally understand the shortfall of her own benefits.

She knew how important insurance was, and she had religiously scheduled annual reviews with her financial professional. But she relied on the financial professional to tell her that everything was in order rather than asking him critical questions. She felt betrayed because the financial professional never taught her, and she felt angry with herself for not demanding to be taught—for delegating it to someone other than herself. She knew that she had short-term disability benefits at her job. But her financial professional never took the time to help her understand the 40-percent shortfall between the benefits and her income and monthly expenses in conjunction with her husband's financial commitments to his children. Maria never asked those critical questions.

Maria felt that no woman should go through the financial stress, physical pain, and emotional devastation that followed surgery. But with the inner grace that had been her strong suit, she was determined to "best this thing," as she called it. She embraced European and Asian therapies, macrobiotics, vegetarianism, and waited.

And she waited.

During her wait, Maria knew she would face an uphill battle with cancer. She would face a financial battle. She would face an emotional battle of not being able to have children of her own. She would face a larger battle with adoption agencies that would not consent to adoption because her health and the demanding hours of her career did not make her a suitable candidate at that time. She faced her company closing and losing her job. But she did not expect to face another woman in her husband's life—and the divorce that resulted.

She waited and would often joke to her closest friends how she "just couldn't wait to turn forty." Everybody else hated the thought of turning forty. Maria was eager for it because on that day it meant that she would have survived cancer seven years in remission.

She dreamed of the fortieth birthday. She had signs in her office and on her refrigerator door, "40 or Bust." Believing she would also face a mastectomy, she didn't know which would come first. Her humor was bizarre, yet always hopeful. She told me how she had planned the morning of her birthday. First, there would be Mass as on every day, followed by a breakfast-meeting celebration. The breakfast meeting would be to purchase disability income insurance—for on that day she would again become insurable. And facing the world alone, she would never again rely on the minimum disability income protection provided by company benefits. Nor would she ever believe that a working husband would ensure that the monthly mortgage and living expenses were paid in the event that she became unable to work.

In April 1992, Maria lived to have her breakfast.

She recalls, "I was smiling like a Cheshire cat the whole way to a breakfast buffet where I heaped bean sprouts and broccoli on my dish. I also placed an à la carte order for $3,000 of monthly disability income protection. I figured it was better for my future than a helping of blintzes."

Maria eventually moved to another position in the corporate world and was comfortable there with all of the benefits—401(k) retirement planning, long-term disability income protection, health insurance, $450,000 of life insurance, and a large salary providing her with $12,000 of monthly income. Her loyalties ran high. She tended to pursue a job and develop it on a track of excellence. She was not a corporate climber or job hopper; therefore, her style was not to pursue a high-profile, "Golden Wonder Boy" strategy up the corporate ladder. Because she was stable with a reputable track record, she believed in job security and envisioned being with the company for years. She had purchased and remodeled a home to her liking in a beautiful area near work.

Maria reached out to me and asked if I felt that she needed to do more, because she never again wanted "to be held hostage" by a passive attitude. I reviewed the individual life insurance and her individual disability income protection coverage that she had purchased three years earlier, and I reviewed the benefits she had with her employer.

During the interview, Maria told me of the cancer she had experienced and how happy she was to be once again "insurable" and qualify for disability income protection. We did an additional fact find to assess her income compared with her expenses. We both agreed that she had adequate disability income coverage provided through her employer plus the individual protection that she had purchased earlier. Yet, she did qualify for higher individual disability income protection based on the fact that her income had skyrocketed.

Before pursuing additional mutual funds and retirement planning, because she was a recovering cancer patient in a high stress job and totally on her own with enormous expenses,

Maria was adamant about first obtaining even more individual disability income protection.

Three years later, Maria found herself in a management regime change that eventually forced her out of the position to which she had devoted her life. She was suddenly faced with no income, no benefits, and unable to pay a monthly fee of $400 for the federally-mandated extended COBRA health benefits. For months, Maria found it difficult to find any job, let alone a position that would ever equal her previous salary.

She called to break the news to me the day that she was told to clean out her desk and leave the office. In the middle of the hurt and confusion of what was happening to her, I reminded her that the individual disability income coverage she had purchased while working cannot ever be canceled as long as she paid the annual premium every year.

Later, Maria told me more about the day she left the promises and benefits of the corporate world—carrying her career and life out the door in a white cardboard file box. In the midst of such confusion, she was proud.

Maria was proud of her sense of personal accountability for her own financial affairs. She was thankful that she knew that the disability income protection she had as an employee benefit was not portable and did not continue when she left the company. But even more, she was proud that when most people at her income level would have been content with one personal income disability policy and would have begun aggressive investing in long-term savings vehicles, Maria's priority instead was to maximize individual disability coverage. She was proud that she truly understood the implications this had for an educated, single women who was unemployed and facing a long road to find another equitable position.

Maria knew that in the near future if she pursued starting her own consulting business, most likely she could not immediately earn a salary at her previous level. Because she would be a start-up business with high expenses and no established track record of income over the next few years, she knew that she could not qualify for any disability coverage. She was gratified that she had such sizable individual disability income protection that would always stay with her.

As a player and pawn on the board of corporate chess, she had escaped capture. Maria was proud that this time in her life, when adversity confronted her, she had made a strategic winning move.

Understanding Your Company Benefits

Before your financial professional can totally assess your financial situation and determine strategies for financial growth, you both must understand the benefits you may or may not have with your company as well as what you can lose if you are no longer with the firm.

My women clients fall into five categories regarding employee benefits. The first are those wage earners with child or elder care responsibilities who can only work part-time and receive no benefits. The second do not work outside the home and rely on their husband's benefits. The third are from dual-income families who are full-time employees or professionals with paid benefits but who claim their spouse's employer as their primary carrier. The fourth are single wage earners who are full-time employees or professionals. Fifth are women business owners with staffs. All agree that they do not fully understand the critical relationship and impact employee benefits have on their future financial strategies.

During a job search campaign, job seekers place great emphasis on obtaining the best benefit package, and the choice of which company to work for is often based on the competitiveness of the benefits. However, the focus on the benefits often stops when the job is landed. Unfortunately, job seekers can often spend more time preparing the résumé and deciding which suit to wear on the interview than understanding their benefits afterwards. As new employees, women are often busy learning company procedures, position requirements, and company politics; they do not take the time to learn all the details of their benefit package. Once joining a new company, many women are satisfied that they have benefits and don't explore them fully until a need or emergency arises. Then it is sometimes too late. Career women often tell me that they consider their company as "family" and have been lulled into thinking of the company as "a father figure adequately taking care of them." Company benefits are sometimes not enough. One plan cannot possibly serve the needs of all.

Over the years, women clients, like Maria, have shared their life's lessons regarding employee benefits. Here are a few:

> "Except for the highest executive level positions in a corporation, benefit packages are usually not negotiable."
>
> —TB

> "For any woman to think that a company benefit package is designed to her personal advantage to help her accumulate wealth is erroneous."
>
> —KLH

> "For anyone to think that company insurance and disability benefits are all they need is naïve. That might only work if you can be at the same company for a lifetime—and those days are long gone in America."
>
> —KMS

> "For any woman to say that her husband's plan 'will take care of it' is short sighted. What if the husband or his job do not last?"
>
> —MS

Disability, divorce, company mergers and consolidations, corporate downsizing, job outplacement, preexisting conditions, changes in occupation, changes in job classification, leaving the corporate world to start your own business—all have a financial impact on the security of your future as well as your protection for the short term. Whether you are staff or upper management, if you are employed with paid benefits through a partnership, small business, corporation, or professional firm, you owe it to yourself to completely understand what *group insurance* benefits you have, what you can lose, and the overall impact this has on your financial program over the long term.

Common basic ingredients in today's corporate benefit packages and their impact on your future planning follow.

Short-Term Disability

For Maria, life changed with a dream. Many people don't think they will ever become disabled. It's nothing you expect. Plus, if you're like most of us, you think accidents and disability are things that happen "to someone else." However, illness and accidents leading to short-term disability are not all that uncommon, and the impact on your income and wealth accumulation could be disastrous.

With a short-term disability, your loss of earnings immediately affects cash flow into your checking account for monthly expenses. The provisions and amount of your short-term disability coverage with an employer determine the size of the short-term savings reservoir necessary for emergencies. Here are key questions that you must answer:

- How long after your illness or injury will it take for your monthly disability income payment to begin?
- What portion of your regular salary will you receive?
- How does the company define "short term" and "disability"?
- Is the premium being paid by the company or are you paying for it by means of payroll deduction?
- Do you have sick days? If so, what portion of your salary is covered if you are out with a short-term illness?
- How are sick days accrued? Do you lose these sick days after a certain length of time if you haven't used them?

There are short-term policies available that go into effect on the first day of an accident or the eighth day of illness. The most common coverage provided by the insurance company will pay a percentage of your income up to sixty days, ninety days or six months. There are policies, however, that define short-term as being up to twelve months. It is very important that you know exactly what these provisions are and how that affects the amount you need in your short-term savings emergency reservoir relative to your monthly expenses for the period as well as unforeseen expenses that may occur due to the disability. It is not unusual for companies to have different levels of provisions based on a person's rank or position within the firm. It is also possible that if you are in a corporate or other non-union environment, there will be no provision for sick days. It is not unusual for only partial salary to be provided in the event that you are sick. *If you're not aware of the details of your benefits, you are liable to make a critical mistake such as having all of your money tied up in non-liquid investment funds without an ample liquid short-term savings reserve because you assumed that your disability income payments would begin immediately or that you would receive full salary.*

How the company defines *disability* is also important. Typically, the definition states that as long as you are unable to perform the regular material duties of your position you are considered to be "disabled" as long as you are not working at any other occupation.

Long-Term Disability

These programs are designed to begin when the maximum benefits period for short-term disability benefits has been reached and benefits are exhausted. Ask the following questions:

- What kind of paperwork is necessary and how long after your illness or injury will it take for your monthly disability income payment to be processed?
- How long after that will your first payment begin?
- What portion of your regular salary will you receive?
- Will bonus income be covered by your disability benefit?
- How does the company define "long term" and "disability"?

If you have a short-term disability program that would have been in effect for six months, then typically the company will have the long-term disability program start after six months and continue anywhere from five years to retirement age. How the company "defines" long-term disability again is very important. With *group disability income programs* through an employer, there can be many stipulations and exclusions to these programs. Such stipulations are not as prevalent if you carry your own noncancelable *personal disability income insurance* protection.

Often *group long-term disability programs* through employers will have a *two-year mental and nervous* benefit. This means that if you should have a nervous breakdown or any illness deriving from mental or nervous conditions, the company's insurance provider would only provide payments for two years.

As Maria learned so well, group disability income protection means that if you leave employment, you cannot take the benefit and protection with you; if it is group coverage, it is not portable. If you become downsized or unemployed, or if you choose to start your own business as a result, you cannot carry the group benefit with you.

Medical Insurance

As in the disability income protection discussion mentioned above, unforeseen medical expenses in addition to the loss of income if you are ill or disabled can lead to financial ruin. Many employers have clauses that preclude coverage based on preexisting medical conditions. Some employers require a six-month waiting period before medical benefits are provided. One client who was the wife of an engineer relayed a story about what happened within six months of her husband's starting his first "real" job following graduate school. At age twenty-eight, he had been having dizzy spells, fell over on the job and was hospitalized. He had tumors on his cranial nerves and needed brain surgery. He was in the hospital for three months, had twenty-seven spinal taps and was unable to work for eighteen months afterward. His illness occurred before the company medical coverage was in effect; their medical bills were more than $250,000. They had been married for one year and lost everything of what little they had. Even if the 80 percent/20 percent copay insurance was available to them, their share of expenses and post-operative care would have totaled $43,000.

It takes a little homework, but learn what your benefits are before you need them. Questions to understand regarding your medical coverage are:

◆ What is your deductible payment before insurance payments begin?
◆ What is your copayment arrangement? That is, what percent does the medical insurance coverage pay and what percent is your responsibility?

- ◆ Understand the definitions within the medical insurance certificate—what it will cover and what it will not cover.
- ◆ Are you eligible for COBRA benefits if you should leave employment and how does it apply to you?

Keep in mind that this COBRA individual medical coverage can be considerably more expensive than the group medical insurance coverage you were receiving while you were employed. If you are outplaced, you must also know that COBRA coverage is necessary in order to maintain an "uninterrupted break" in medical coverage. If you have no coverage, and it takes you nine months to a year to find adequate employment, it could seriously impact you if you become disabled or develop a medical condition before your new company benefits are in effect; it would be considered a preexisting condition and exempt from coverage in many cases. The financial consequences can be even larger if you are a long-tenured, highly paid, technical or professional employee for whom it may take a considerable amount of time to secure a comparable position.

Your financial professional can help you calculate the impact these circumstances will have on your ability to pay expenses and what additional sums need to be placed in your short-term savings reserve.

Social Security

You may not give much thought to Social Security if you are far from retirement age. Under Social Security, employees qualify for benefit payments based on a certain number of work credits. Once you have enough credits, your benefit amount depends on your average earnings over your working lifetime.

As of the publication of this book, the Social Security program was the focus of intense debate and the shape of its future is unclear. But Social Security does provide more than retirement benefits; it also provides important disability, family, and survivor benefits. As you approach retirement age, become disabled, or lose a spouse or parent who supports you, you should inquire about the benefits that might be available to you.

It is also wise to check with the Social Security Administration every few years to verify that your earnings are accurately recorded. This can be done by obtaining a "Request for Earnings and Benefit Estimate Statement" from your local Social Security office. It takes a few minutes to complete. You will receive a written statement for your records. You can also obtain this information online by visiting the Social Security Administration's web site.

Social Security benefits are generally discounted as mythic among financial professionals who are serious about helping their clients achieve true financial success.

Pensions and Investments

More attention is paid to the accumulation benefits of an employer than the protection benefits—simply because these are more fun. Obtain answers to the following questions:

- ♦ Does your employer offer a 401(k), 403(b), or other type of retirement plan?
- ♦ With a 401(k), does the company match your contribution?
- ♦ If it is a matching situation, how much does the company match?
- ♦ Are you maximizing your employee contributions in your 401(k)?
- ♦ What is your account worth?
- ♦ In what type of funds are you presently investing?
- ♦ Are you monitoring your accounts quarterly and discussing it with your financial professional?

Monitoring your quarterly reports or annual statements will help you feel the pleasure and witness the potential growth that can result from disciplined savings over time. Fully understanding your 401(k) or 403(b) plan is not only knowing the extent to which you are making contributions, but also understanding how the different funds are performing. Monitoring the growth of your account and the diversification of funds in which your dollars are distributed is just as important as the amounts you are putting into your account. Different rates of return are earned by different fund performances.

The *Rule of 72* is commonly used in the financial services industry. (It means that if you want your money to double within a certain number of years, you divide 72 by the number of years. The result gives you the rate of interest you need to earn on your money. Conversely, if you divide 72 by the rate of interest you are already earning, it will tell you how long it will take to double your money.)

For example, assuming a 5-percent interest rate is maintained, your fund could double in just over fourteen years. It is important to note that when dealing with investments there is no guarantee. Values will fluctuate.

Therefore, as you monitor your retirement account, you want to watch the rates of return you are getting on your various fund accounts as well as what funds you are choosing. The company pension accounts should be reviewed quarterly with your financial professional who can assist you in selecting the most appropriate funds for your 401(k) or 403(b) program to position your portfolio for maximum earnings based on your risk tolerance. It is your responsibility to be proactive.

Life Insurance

Group term insurance is considered an inexpensive benefit. A face amount two or three times your annual salary is common in the employee benefits arena. This type of insurance generally provides death benefit protection only. Furthermore, many group contracts are available to your beneficiary only if you die while you are working. (Some pension plans also continue term insurance benefits.) Most group term insurance is not portable; if your firm downsizes and you become outplaced, or you develop an illness that makes you uninsurable, you cannot take the term insurance with you when you leave the firm. Some insurance companies may provide an opportunity for you to convert group life insurance into a permanent life insurance policy.

Here is what you should ask about your *group term insurance* program:

- How many times (1x, 2x, 3x) your salary is provided?
- What is the shortfall of death benefit protection between what you have with your group coverage vs. what you need to adequately protect your family?
- Calculate the difference to determine the extent to which you are underinsured.
- Is any type of life insurance part of the company retirement package?

Employee benefits are a detailed and complex arena of understanding. Make sure all questions you have about benefits are answered in writing by a officer of your firm, or are documented in your firm's benefit handbook published for associates of the company. Each time you change firms, it is necessary to address changes in your group benefits and determine any adjustments you need to make to your short-term liquid savings account as well as your long-term insurance and investment portfolios.

A summary of all group benefits that you have with your firm is necessary for a complete analysis of your financial program. Your financial professional can assess all your current funds in relationship to the future and, at your next meeting, take time to explain how these group benefits need to be coordinated with your individual insurance and investment programs to help accomplish your long-term goals.

STEP 9
Coordinating Company and Personal Planning

Critical Mix of Protection

The corporate, private business, and professional worlds bring great benefits. Now that you understand the value of risk protection and investment growth you have with your firm, it is time for you and your financial professional to help you understand and coordinate the critical mix of protection necessary between group benefits and what you have as an individual to accomplish your long-term goals.

When your long-term goal is wealth accumulation, a basic premise is that after you are free of significant debt, *protection comes first*. That means protection of your income stream as well as your personal or business assets. No real financial growth can occur if either cash flow or assets are in jeopardy. Let's look at areas of vulnerability where group benefits can fall short of your total needs and where private individual protection needs to be supplemented.

Property and Casualty Insurance

For most Americans, the first type of insurance they obtain is property and casualty insurance (P&C) to protect an auto; this is followed by renter's or homeowner's insurance. My clients normally do not consider property and casualty insurance to be a part of their long-term planning, nor do they feel that it has any relationship at all to the benefits they may have with their company. But here is one critical aspect to consider. No true long-term financial program can be secure if you are personally exposed to loss of assets because of exposure to liability.

Many property and casualty insurance companies offer *personal*, *professional* and/or *commercial umbrella policies* to provide very high limits of excess liability coverage. If you are a parent with teenage children who drive, it is wise to have maximum liability protection. There are scores of heartbreaking stories regarding a teenage son or daughter who is the driver in an auto or boating accident that disfigures, or kills a child, another teenager, or pedestrian. If alcohol or substance abuse are also involved, the personal lawsuits, court cases, and financial liabilities can devastate and ruin growing families.

People with high profile positions can also be accused of defamation of character, invasion of privacy, libel, or slander. Professionals such as physicians, financial professionals, teachers, lawyers, accountants, druggists, real estate agents, and architects, just to name a few, can obtain professional umbrella policies. Liability insurance for these individuals is also known as *malpractice insurance* or *errors and omissions* insurance, and it seeks to indemnify the professional for malpractice, mistakes, or errors committed or alleged to have been committed while performing professional duties.

Various types of commercial liability protection can be obtained if you are a business owner and the nature of your business exposes you to liability such as libel, slander, defamation, unfair competition, idea misappropriation, and the like.

Various types of umbrella policies can offer additional protection. Not all umbrella policies are the same. You should work closely with your property and casualty agent to carefully determine what coverage and type of policy will be the most beneficial regarding your type of risk exposure.

Qualified employee retirement plans are protected from general creditors. Cash value life insurance and annuities (in some states) may also be entitled to protection. Assets that are exposed to general creditors include mutual funds, stocks, bonds, and certificates of deposit that are not within a qualified employee retirement plan. It is important that your professional team be in contact with your property and casualty agent to ensure that the values of *all* of your assets, in addition to your home, are taken into consideration when considering the correct amount of liability coverage necessary for you. You should always check with your attorney regarding the types of property protected from creditors in your jurisdiction.

Disability Income Protection

Between individual and group coverage, you are allowed approximately 60-70 percent of your gross income to be protected by disability income insurance. This puts you at a 30-40 percent shortfall in the event that you experience illness or disability; if you are relying on 10 percent for savings, your ability to accumulate savings is immediately thrown into jeopardy. For example, with a $100,000 income, the insurance companies would allow you up to 70 percent of your annual income, or $70,000 of annual disability income coverage.

As a side note, you should be aware that major changes are currently afoot in the disability income insurance marketplace. Many companies no longer offer this coverage because a large volume of claims is causing them extraordinary losses. Therefore, contract language is changing dramatically. For instance, at one time individual disability income policies had a lifetime *mental and nervous* provision; today that has been altered by many companies, some with a two-year or less maximum benefit period.

If a long-term disability program is offered as an employment benefit, you would lose the income replacement protection if you lost your position or chose to leave the firm. Therefore, it is wise to consider having an additional individual disability policy in order to maximize what is allowed. Your individual disability income protection policy is controlled by you because you are personally paying the premium and you will never lose coverage or protection as long as you pay your annual premium.

If 70 percent is the maximum coverage allowable in the event of a disability, it is advisable to become accustomed to living on 70 percent of your gross income. Put the remaining 30 percent away on a monthly basis to have available for emergency needs and wealth accumulation.

Another advantage to individual disability income programs has to do with taxes. Employer paid coverage is taxable income to you. However, if you own a non-cancelable individual policy, your benefit will be tax free.

For entrepreneurs without group benefits, individual coverage can be vital. Jim was out with his family on a Sunday afternoon at the lake. He tripped and fell off the pier and crushed his right hip. A visit to the clinic determined that surgery was needed. Because Jim was self-employed, the business couldn't operate without his presence; the injury prevented him from working for six months. His family relied on his income for the house payment, food and clothing, and utilities. Jim and Ellen had enough in their short-term savings to carry the business overhead as well as the household for three months. Expenses for the following three months were supported by his individual disability income protection policy. Jim was lucky because he and Ellen planned. However, he and Ellen still faced the worry of losing contracts and customers because of his absence.

Another case concerns Ann, who is a psychologist, single, with a full patient load. She was happy and secure with her life when she experienced a severe auto accident. After months of therapy and having to cut back on seeing patients due to severe back pain, she was advised to have back surgery followed by more rest. Ann was fortunate to have an individual disability income policy that helped replace her income and assisted her in paying her personal expenses. However, Ann did not have a disability overhead expense program to pay for expenses at her professional office. She needed to cash in her IRA accounts to support the business expenses of $1,500 per month for seven months due to a lag time in receivables. Ann was fortunate to have a $20,000 IRA account to cover the $10,500. However, her penalties were substantial. If Ann had had a business overhead expense policy, she could have left her IRA in place. She had no spouse or family who could help her. She worried about not being available to her patients and about being healthy enough to resume her patient work. Ann's total time away from her practice was five months.

Life Insurance

Life insurance is such a common benefit that group term insurance can be overrated and misunderstood as well. It is important to realize that term insurance carries death benefit protection only and accumulates no cash values. It is a wonderful benefit—if you are working.

Let's consider these common scenarios that are witnessed in my practice every week. Your management position at your company is redefined and rewritten, as many are in corporate America. With no union or advocate to protect your interests, your position is eliminated; you no longer have the coverage. You are now looking for other work. Under the stress during the months of the outplacement process, you may develop a condition or illness that causes you to lose your insurability, and you cannot get insurance. Another common situation occurs if you have been working outside the home for thirty or so. It may be close to retirement time; suddenly you realize that you will outlive your job and have no insurance, plus you discover that term insurance is not extended as part of your retirement package. At age sixty or sixty-five, you would face a high insurance premium at a time when you have lost your earning power; perhaps you even may be uninsurable for health reasons.

These are only a few reasons why everyone should consider a properly designed insurance program that mixes group and individual coverages. When women first visit me for guidance, it has been frightening to see how many women have insurance only through their employer or firm. If you have diabetes, or have heart or stress problems that are documented through your medical coverage, or have a major illness and lose insurability, you may not be able to get any more insurance at the time of leaving the firm.

The additional life insurance program needs to be diversified so the premium can be easily accommodated with your discretionary income. Also consider the benefit of having a permanent life insurance program by the time you wish to retire, rather than just beginning one! For many, it does not make sense to have term insurance without cash value at work and also have an individually owned term insurance policy—unless you are aggressively putting money away on a monthly basis outside of work as well.

That is to say if your accumulation program has not reached the point where you are placing monthly contributions to additional mutual funds or other investment vehicles, cash value insurance that can accumulate cash values over time is generally preferred over additional term insurance.

With our American culture and lifestyle expectations, the need for life insurance never goes away. If life insurance is analyzed in terms of cost outlay and return of premium, cash value type life insurance will generally be better economically over the long term. If we knew when we were going to die, then term insurance would probably be a very good buy from an economic standpoint.

Pension and Investments

Retirement plans such as 401(k) or 403(b) are excellent if you can take full advantage of them. Your benefit department will inform you of the amount of money you are allowed to contribute to this program on a *pre-tax basis*. (This means that you pay tax on your income after the contribution has been made.) If an employer is matching 3 percent in your 401(k) and you are saving 3 percent, that means that 6 percent of the gross income is being saved on a monthly basis for future retirement. Income that does not pass through your hands through such payroll deduction or deposit methods is unavailable for you to spend. That helps ensure it will go toward your future goals. Over time, such savings from even modest salaries can amount to hundreds of thousands of dollars.

Investments in 401(k) or 403(b) plans are portable if you lose your position or leave the firm. Whatever you have accumulated can be *rolled over* into an individual retirement (IRA) account or to your employer's plan for the purpose of avoiding taxes on the sum when you leave the firm. In the meantime, your investment reserve can continue to grow in a diversified portfolio and be available when you reach a government-specified age. When you retire and are ready to use the monthly income, you then pay current income tax on the accumulated amount based on your income tax bracket. Such retirement plans are forced accumulation vehicles with distinct tax advantages.

At this point you have a better understanding of what you can lose when you lose group benefits. You should know why it is necessary for individual insurance and investment programs to coordinate with your group benefits. You know that you must calculate your short-term savings to cover shortfalls in personal and business cash flow that is left unprotected. If you are an entrepreneur, you should also know that both your personal cash flow as well as your business overhead need to be protected. These are three important principles in protecting your earnings stream and existing assets and savings from jeopardy. When you have addressed these, you are well on your way to having the confidence of knowing that you are protected from financial jeopardy due to risk and that protection will enable you to begin *aggressively* pursuing your desire for wealth accumulation.

STEP 10

Learning How to Diversify Savings, Insurance and Investments for Now and the Future

Diversification

Now you're at the point where you understand the need to protect your cash flow and assets while you plan an aggressive financial strategy. The next logical question is what do I do now? You're waiting for an analysis of your financial condition and recommendations.

All future planning must first consider the time period required to achieve a goal. *Short-term goals* are defined as one-through five-year goals. *Intermediate goals* are six through ten year goals. *Long-term goals* are more than ten years until the projected time when the money is needed.

As mentioned above, debt reduction and building short-term savings for emergency funds are generally considered short-term needs. Long-term needs are those such as retirement, funding a college education, paying off a mortgage, business succession arrangements, estate tax needs, leaving a legacy to heirs, insurance for the purpose of charitable giving to a religious, medical, or art institution, and the like. It is important to select the proper funding vehicles so that you are not subject to surrender fees or sizable loss due to market fluctuations.

I am reminded of a client who told me a story about her plan to accumulate money for a three- to five-year period for a down payment to purchase her first home on her own. Karyn was young and out of college, totally trusting, and wasn't comfortable asking many questions. The agent who was selling her auto insurance suggested that she begin placing her money in an annuity; this Karyn did. The agent totally lost sight of Karyn's need to withdraw the money in three to five years. For her purpose, an annuity was an inappropriate product to accomplish her goal. As we have seen, annuities are designed as long-term investment products designed for retirement. When Karyn proceeded to take her money out of her annuity to buy her house, she was devastated to be charged substantial IRS withdrawal penalties. Mutual funds would have been a better choice for her.

It's time for you to come to grips with the jargon you'll hear on that next interview with your financial professional. Don't worry! It's okay to be clueless. The insurance and the investment world is complicated. It takes years for your financial professional to learn and apply knowledge. So do not be embarrassed about what you do not understand. It's a must for you to ask questions and share your feelings. Your financial professional is there to teach you. After all, that's what you are paying for! If all you wanted was to purchase a product, you could do it by mail—as you do with catalogue purchases. Remember, you are in control. If it seems that the financial professional is not explaining financial concepts in a way that you understand, just stop; slow down the conversation and ask questions—many questions. Even if you feel secure in knowing what's available in the financial marketplace for your personal needs, perhaps you are contemplating starting your own business. The world of insurance and investments for business needs is another world—equally complex.

People who have accumulated sizeable assets generally both understand and adhere to the concept of *portfolio diversification*. (This means that your total financial program incorporates life insurance, mutual funds, stocks, bonds, and/or other investments.) Diversification requires a fundamental understanding that each of the various products in the financial marketplace is designed differently to accomplish certain goals. Some are more appropriate for certain needs than others. Some may be totally inappropriate. Remember that diversitication reduces, but does not eliminate the risk of experiencing losses.

So let's learn from Karyn and go back to the classroom. Our objective isn't to learn all the details and features of every product in the financial marketplace. That's the domain of your professional team. But you do want to acquire a broad understanding of the types of products available. One client used an analogy that I will remember forever. She equated the diversification process to learning about fabrics. Denim is strong, sturdy, and hot. It's great for western riding wear, but you wouldn't wear it to work in a professional office setting. Pima cotton breathes and is absorbent; it's best suited for hot climates, but you wouldn't want a winter coat made of it. Polyester needs no ironing, wears well and is lightweight, but you wouldn't select it for your wedding dress. All fabrics work best for the purpose for which they are tailored. Chances are that your wardrobe contains denim, cotton, polyester, wool, silk, and linen (among others)—diverse fabrics for a variety of needs. The same holds true with tailoring a diversified financial portfolio.

Now, let's go to class.

Diversification 101

Keep in mind, this is a quick survey of the types of vehicles that you might find available. There may also be others. Be certain to discuss them in detail with your financial professional, who is qualified to teach you about how each product works and what it can or cannot achieve relative to your individual needs.

There are many concepts to consider when making decisions about accumulating money based on your goal or purpose for having the money. Your personal or business needs determine how the portfolio should be diversified. There is not one single product or investment that is designed to be a total answer for short- and long-term needs, wants, and desires. If the goal is to have a short-term savings account that can be easily accessible for emergency needs, there are several ways to accomplish this. These can include an interest-paying money market account with a checkbook, a bank savings account, saving through credit union payroll deduction, and a certificate of deposit.

Depending on your ability to pay and the time available to accomplish your goals, designing a properly diversified portfolio can help satisfy your needs. When you begin to contribute to stocks, bonds, and mutual funds, a professional *risk tolerance questionnaire* must be completed to analyze how much you are willing to risk at various returns, with various levels of guarantee

including no guarantee. (*American Dream Women: A Workbook &*
Planning Guide provides a detailed questionnaire and explanation.) The process of investing in mutual funds, stocks, and bonds
differs from investing in certificates of deposit because CDs are
FDIC insured and offer a guaranteed rate of return; however,
investment in securities will fluctuate.

STEP 11
Controlling the Buying Process

Being in the Know

Some of my women clients would tell me about their fear of making a buying decision. Many just "freeze" when it comes time to decide. All agree that they rarely want "to sign anything" on a first interview and that they want "to take time to think about it." I often hear, "I've read and learned a little about mutual funds and insurance, but how do I know what my financial professional is recommending is right for me?"

Demand to Be Taught

Understanding key financial concepts goes a long way toward building your confidence. Demand study materials and start the process of learning. As mentioned at the outset, asking questions and learning before making decisions is the way most women should buy; so do not skip this process.

Instead, get excited and feel good because you have become responsible; you are in control. You are no longer a passenger; you are in the driver's seat. Consider it just as you do when buying a car. The research, the decision, and the final choice about how the vehicle fits your short-term and long-term needs are yours. You are going to be paying for the car, and you are going to own it. The same is true of each vehicle in your portfolio. It's time to get tough. Treat your financial future the same as if you were buying your car or your house—treat it like a major purchase that will have long-lasting consequences. In truth, your financial decisions have even longer consequences—far longer than any choice about your wardrobe, your house, your car, and yes, even the choice about your life partner.

Turn fright into might by being in the know. It's time women turn their timidity about financial affairs into action. An angry widow once told me, "For years men have been making decisions about family and retirement finances. Yet, women outlive men; therefore, we must live with those decisions."

At this point in the process, you should be ready for a second interview to hear recommendations. You have considered your current situation as well as wants, needs, and dreams for your future. Recap the planning you have accomplished to this point and ensure your final selection fits your goals.

- ♦ You know and have listed each of your monthly expenses and debt load for your household as well as your business.
- ♦ You have calculated your short-term savings for emergency protection needs to cover your overhead and expenses for a three- to six-month period.
- ♦ You have listed your personal short- and long-term desires.
- ♦ You understand what insurance protection you already have to protect your assets: home, personal property, earning and income stream, business cash flow, business continuation, life and estate.
- ♦ You have ensured that an up-to-date will has been prepared that states your wishes for your family and beneficiaries in the event of your death.
- ♦ You understand the results of your risk tolerance questionnaire.
- ♦ You understand what value the dollar might have when you are retirement age.
- ♦ You have begun to calculate the cost of your lifestyle needs at retirement.
- ♦ You have calculated how much you must save based on your expected rate of return to satisfy your wants, needs, and desires.
- ♦ You have determined if and how you need to alter your saving and spending patterns to accomplish your goals over the next 10, 15, 20, 25, or 30 years.
- ♦ You have demanded that your financial professional explains the role of each product in your current portfolio and how it addresses your goals for the long term.

♦ You have demanded that your financial professional explain any *additional* recommendations and products that you may purchase in terms of your plans for the future.

Whatever your time allows, it is necessary that you demand that your financial professional teach you how the pieces in your portfolio work together to accomplish your protection and accumulation goals. This can help ensure that your portfolio is diversified and in your best interests. The one most important thing you can do is ask questions, ask more questions and then ask again. You must demand that you be taught.

Demand Communication among Your Professional Team

Do not assume that what a financial professional recommends is what you need. Perhaps a financial professional is not licensed to sell you what you really need. You should feel comfortable and certain that you are part of the sales process and that your life, your occupation, your expenses, what kinds of risks you are willing to take with your money, your dreams, and your desires have been considered. You should feel with great confidence that your financial program has been designed for only you. A single woman who has benefits as an employee in the corporate world has different needs than a married or divorced woman attempting to educate children through college. The right recommendations and proposed strategies to help ensure asset protection and your accumulation goals depend on your lifestyle. Therefore, you should not get the feeling that your financial professional sells the same product and the same amount to everyone.

On the second interview, if your financial professional seems to be impatient with you for asking questions or gives you answers that you still do not understand, then most likely your best interests are not being met and the relationship will not last for the long term. Again, here is yet another step where you can feel lucky that you've seen the light before a buying decision has been made. As mentioned before, recommending that your financial professional communicate decisions with your

CPA and your attorney creates another set of checks and balances and *professional accountability* among your professional team that is sure to serve *your* best interests.

If you are satisfied that your financial professional, in conjunction with your CPA and attorney, have attended to the items listed above, then you have developed a confidence that they are working in your best interests.

At this point, let's assume that you and your financial professional concur on what you need to secure your protection and accumulation needs and the appropriate products to consider based on those needs. We now complete the cycle of decision making and the final two steps in the process—purchasing a product, committing to review your progress over the long term, and making adjustments when necessary.

STEP 12
Selecting a Company and Product

Does the Company Really Matter?

Women buy based on relationships first, and then they should be confident that the company whose product they choose is strong, stable, and reputable. Men more often follow the challenge of a "hot lead" to invest in a new product or maverick business venture. The majority of women I've serviced in my career take a more conservative approach.

You ought to feel comfortable about the company you choose. Many companies that have been around for a hundred years or more have demonstrated that they can weather the strong currents, tides, and storms of economic cycles. Whereas a company that has been established for ten years may not have yet demonstrated a similar ability to remain steadfast through economic hardship.

There are many questions to ask your financial professional about the company and the product you plan to purchase:

- ♦ Given the product you are purchasing, is there marketing information that discusses its performance over time and how it compares with similar products in the marketplace?
- ♦ If it is a company whose name you are not familiar with, have you checked with your state insurance department about whether the company is licensed in your state?
- ♦ If you are considering mutual funds or securities, what is their 3-, 5- or 10-year past performance, including sales charges?
- ♦ What is the company's philosophy about service? Can you call the company directly with questions or must you go through the local office?
- ♦ What is the company's main product emphasis? In what does the company excel?

♦ What technical expertise does the company offer your financial professional?

As we come to the close of the process, you can feel confident in knowing that you now have an insider's view of the fundamentals of a diversified planning process. It is a process that advocates an active relationship between you and your team of professionals.

Remember, neither a twelve-step process nor the personal financial program a woman creates can succeed on its own. Success requires personal accountability, commitment, discipline, and periodic review. Think of it as you would overseeing the maintenance of your car. There can be serious consequences if the oil and other vital fluids are not checked on a regular basis. There can be serious or fatal consequences if the tires are not properly inflated, rotated, or changed. Waiting to attend to your vehicle until after it breaks makes you vulnerable and places you in jeopardy. The vehicle will not perform to its optimum without periodic monitoring and service. Your service station will oblige if you take the car in for servicing—they cannot help you unless you are proactive and request the service. Remember, you are in the driver's seat.

The analogy applies to monitoring the performance of your investment vehicles as well. Your financial portfolio requires frequent review. Because the investment marketplace is dynamic and fluctuating, if you are investing in a diversified portfolio, you must be involved and aware. Review each annual policy statement or fund statement when you receive it; don't just file it in a folder in your desk! You must understand how the funds are performing. Feel comfortable to call your financial professional to teach you how to read your statements if you are confused.

Investment values are just one aspect of your program needing frequent review. It is also necessary to make certain that the amount of insurance coverage increases to match the need. One example I have witnessed involved a company that chose to have a buy-sell agreement created among three partners. They had $250,000 life insurance on each partner for the intent that if one partner should die, the $250,000 would help pay the family of the partner to buy out the business interest. Because the partners were busy with the details of daily business, there was no time to have an annual review done. The partners did not increase the insurance amount or the buy-out price to keep pace with the value of the growing business. One partner died and the spouse received $250,000 instead of the current value of the partner's interest in the business which had grown to $750,000, which was the amount that the deceased partner would have hoped for the family.

I recommend that insurance be reviewed on an annual basis. Throughout the years of my insurance practice, in an effort to keep my clients' future planning and insurance up-to-date and to provide the best possible service, I have developed materials to teach, communicate, and service clients over the lifetime of our relationship. Since the 1980s, my follow-up letters, ongoing teaching materials, and annual review checklists have helped many clients and families to stay focused on their goals and to update their programs for the future. It gives me great pride to have shared my "client for life" philosophy with my industry associates.

In order to assist you in the twelve-step process to gain control of your financial future, the SeebeckSuccessSystem™ (included in *American Dream Women: A Workbook & Planning Guide*), is designed to make the ongoing annual review and updating of your financial program a habit—one designed to positively impact you for many years to come.

The Importance of Naming a Beneficiary

Another reason for the importance of annual review of your insurance program is to review the beneficiary designations on your policies. The people you name when you purchase your insurance do not necessarily remain your same choices throughout the years. Here are examples of circumstances that have occurred when clients do not update beneficiaries assigned to their insurance policies:

♦ The effect of divorce on the status of a named beneficiary will vary depending on state law. You should always contact your financial professional when the relationship of the beneficiary changes. During the divorce process, request to be rightsholder of his policy. Change the beneficiary on the policy, list yourself as ex-spouse, and submit changes to the insurance company.

- If a business owner purchases a policy for the purpose of covering a business loan at the bank, there is a *collateral assignment* of the policy to the bank. If the loan is paid off, the financial professional has not been notified and the insured dies, and the bank never returned the policy, the family faces time and expense to prove that they are entitled to receive the proceeds of the life insurance policy. Legally, the insurance company must pay the bank as the named beneficiary or receive a signed note from the bank to surrender the money to the family.

- If you have a personal financial professional, but purchase insurance by mail or through an employer, you should notify the financial professional and your family about the policy. It is possible that because your financial professional does not know about the policy your family will never receive the proceeds because the mail-order company many not be aware of the death.

- If an "estate" is named as the beneficiary rather than a spouse or family member, it will delay the family's receipt of the benefit payment if no will was registered.

- A trust and legal will are put in order for a family. The attorney assumes that the insured notified the financial professional to properly design the insurance program along with naming the trust as beneficiary of the policies. All beneficiary changes should be properly documented with the insurance company.

Having defined goals, assessed your current financial condition, created a financial program, implemented it in a series of steps, and committed yourself to periodic review, you now have a quality track to run on that is flexible to adjust with personal circumstances through all cycles of your life.

Now let us look at twelve needs and appropriate strategies that are common throughout various stages in the life of an American woman.

PART II
Eleven Common Needs and Strategies

Throughout my practice, I've serviced hundreds of women who have expressed common needs, wants, and desires for the future. Often, women gain additional confidence by sharing and comparing their situation and goals with those of other women from similar life circumstances.

The second part of this book is dedicated exclusively to a discussion of the common desires of American women who have defined the American Dream in their own terms. These women's stories are organized according to common needs and strategies. In these stories, which are composites of many experiences, women discuss their mistakes along the way, their new goals, and how they are accomplishing them. You are sure to find many parallels with the current stage of life you are in and what you choose for your future. The stories are also organized according to life cycles. If you are like most of our readers, you will read the story that fits your current lifestyle or concern for the future and go back to the others as your life changes.

Each story is independent and complete on its own; it provides background, gives questions to ask, discusses relevant financial needs and legal issues, and poses possible strategies. The need is a lack of something required or desirable in the pursuit of financial success. Necessity greatly intensifies urgency to the point that the need, obligation or requirement cannot be ignored. Exigency stresses great urgency brought about by particular circumstances, which are imposed by external requirements rather than by an inner compulsion. The questions analyze or examine the problem and are those you should readily discuss with your financial professionals. The strategy is a method or process of solving the need. There can be many strategies depending on your personal circumstances; however, these stories present those most common among the women I work with in my practice.

For instructional purposes throughout, my examples use compound interest tables, and average an assumed 5-percent annual rate of return over the time period. The examples do not take into account any charges, fees, or tax considerations. Due to market fluctuation, past performance is not a guarantee of future results, and there is no guarantee of future results; personal results will vary.

1

To Become Debt Free

Single College Grad

— Chen Li —

Chen Li has been having fun. At age twenty-seven, she is a bright, petite, spirited, third-generation Asian-American working her way up the career ladder in a professional firm where she earns a $60,000 starting salary as a promising attorney. Chen Li graduated magna cum laude from Catholic University of America and earned honors distinction and a law degree at Georgetown University in Washington DC, where she served on the *Law Review* editorial board.

Chen Li was referred to me by her former professor and mentor, who is an attorney specializing in intellectual property law in New York. When Chen Li and I began our association, she was quick to point out, "My annual salary is far more than my father ever dreamed of making; if you don't count his car and mortgage, I've also accumulated more debt than he and mother ever had in their lives."

Chen Li explained that she enjoyed spending because her college days were a struggle without money from the family. After graduating from the rigors of law school, she took three months off with classmates from Georgetown to tour Europe and the Far East visiting her great grandparents' homeland in China and spending a great deal of time in Peking. The trip cost her $10,000, which she charged on credit cards. She said, "We worked hard for seven years in college and were determined to enjoy the wonders of the world and go to places we always dreamed of."

Over an eighteen-month period after beginning her new job, Chen Li had accumulated $18,000 of debt. She rented a condominium in a "safe" upscale Washington suburb and charged another $3,000 for furnishings. A designer wardrobe "that was of the caliber that the firm expected" cost her another $5,000, which she also deferred paying for with credit cards. She was thankful she had no student loans to repay.

By age twenty-seven, the thrill of having money and the duty of spending was no longer a reward. Chen Li recalled, "Already, I felt trapped by my own success. The money was there in black and white, but I didn't have any and started to feel suffocated, ashamed and hopelessly in debt. I couldn't imagine what it would be like if I were to marry. If both of us had debt along with student loans my fiancé might have to repay, we could face a potential of $75,000 to $100,000 of debt between us." Chen Li wanted to use the discipline that she had learned throughout her academic studies and at home to help solve her financial worries. She needed to change her life, but did not know where or how to begin.

Needs

After our meeting, Chen Li realized she must begin at the beginning and first understand where her money was being spent by analyzing her expenses, debts, and savings habits. In addition, she needed a budget. She also needed an attitude shift regarding her spending on items she felt "obligated to purchase." Like Chen Li, many women feel similar pressures to spend due to great urgency imposed by external job or peer requirements. Such exigency spending is justified intellectually, but creates a hidden debt addiction and interrupts personal cash flow each month. Chen Li needed to protect her income stream and grow an emergency fund. Plus, she needed to begin an aggressive approach to paying off her debt.

Questions to Ask

If, like Chen Li, you are faced with similar circumstances and wish to aggressively eliminate debt, here are issues you must resolve:

- ♦ Are you willing to begin cash-only spending and put your credit cards away?
- ♦ Do you have any additional major expenses coming up such as a new car purchase?
- ♦ Do you know what is a realistic time frame for you to pay off your debt?
- ♦ Are you willing to cut back on spontaneous purchases and commit yourself to a monthly budget?
- ♦ Will you be receiving any additional salary increases, bonuses, or gifts?
- ♦ Do you have a disability income protection program? Do you know what percent of your salary will be covered? When do the benefits begin?
- ♦ Do you have short-term savings to use as an emergency fund?

Chen's Strategy

The irony in Chen Li's life is that "not having money" is not her dilemma. Her hurdle is having a mindset focused on short-term expenses that she feels obligated to make immediately. As a new attorney, she explained, "the exigencies of my job forced me into an upscale lifestyle, living in an affluent neighborhood, and maintaining an appropriate and honorable image." Her challenge was embracing cash-only spending habits.

Chen Li desired to be debt free as soon as possible and was willing to sacrifice and adhere to cash-only spending. Her two major credit cards were retained. To avoid binge spending, she literally froze her spending by placing the cards in a glass of water in the freezer.

Because of her salary, Chen Li has applied for her own disability income protection policy, knowing that if she is injured and qualifies for benefits, she will receive a monthly check to help pay her bills as well as cover the amount she hoped to begin saving. Her short-term disability income protection would cover her for the first ninety days. Chen Li also was committed to save her bonuses for two years to accumulate $10,000 in a short-term savings account for emergency needs. After that goal is accomplished, she will maximize contributions to her 401(k) retirement plan.

To eliminate her $18,000 debt, we identified her fixed monthly expenses of $3,600, of which $2,200 covered rent, utilities, car payment, and her insurance; she averaged $600 monthly for entertainment, new clothing purchases, etc. Also, $800 was spent each month on payments for two major credit cards as well as several smaller department store credit accounts. She had been spending $9,600 a year to pay off an $18,000 credit card debt. Unfortunately, a portion of her payments were applied to interest rather than paying off the principal.

Chen Li also needed a focused lifestyle change regarding her $600 monthly outlay for entertainment, clothing, and extras. She embraced cash-only spending. She would limit her extras to enable her to apply an additional $500 each month to double credit card payments and to increase payments toward principal. As each card was paid off, she would apply that payment allocation toward increasing payments to another card. Her program would enable her to be debt free as well as accumulate a short-term money market account as an emergency fund in two and a half to three years.

The greatest payoff for Chen Li will come after her debt is eliminated. She will then start aggressive long-term savings, for she will have mastered disciplined spending habits to avoid debt accumulation. The $800 plus $500 she used monthly to pay off credit cards will begin accumulating as savings. If she maintains her discipline, her $15,600 annual contribution to an investment account could potentially yield about $537,000 in twenty years if she is fortunate enough to average an assumed 5-percent annual rate of return without considering charges, fees, or tax implications.

Chen Li admits that initially the discipline of cash-only spending was hard because she "was accustomed to sharing the blessings" of a good salary to help her family and buying what was needed when it was needed. Such generosity was how she demonstrated honor to her parents as a result of achieving "the big job after law school." But when she learned a new definition of her financial power in terms of savings and wealth accumulation rather than spending, it "became easier." She remembered, "I felt good; for the first time, the control of my financial future was in my court."

2

To Save More Money

— Holly —

Holly's father was a hard-working, large hunk of a man with thick black hair and huge hands of taut callused skin; he made a living as a Texas oil rigger. Her mother was a strawberry blonde beauty, thin and frail, who worked as a cook at the local Holiday Inn after their three children went off to grade school. When Holly and I first met, she was twenty. She told me with great pride and sadness that, as her parents raised their family, they found that, no matter how hard they worked, they were stretching paychecks from Friday to Friday, but never getting ahead or able to save. She recalled that the whole family would sit on the porch swings at night telling stories and drinking her mother's homemade lemonade. On special nights, under the hot Texas moon, the kids would make pink lemonade by floating a maraschino cherry on their lemon. Her parents would tell of their dreams of owning a herd of mustangs on a little Texas ranch by the time they were forty-five. Holly's voice cracked as she told me that those dreams were getting more distant the older her parents became. Holly recalled how her parents called "being forty-five" a "magic age when everything would be easy," and they would sit back and raise horses and a few Texas longhorns.

At twenty, Holly was determined to make her own dreams happen. She said, "I just don't know what to do or how to do it." Holly's strength was in knowing *what* she was capable of and doing that with a spirit "to be the best." Even more important at her age was that she knew what she did not know and sought help to make up for what she called her "short sights." Academics was not in her heart; after graduating from high school, Holly chose to "follow a path of beauty." She worked as a waitress as she put herself through cosmetology school with a goal of owning her own salon someday. She graduated with honors; her attitude and sights were set to be the best in her field. Our relationship began shortly thereafter when she started her first job in cosmetology.

Everything Holly does and every move she makes speaks of beauty and grace. Her glossy red hair is cut in a perfect bob that fits her face and freckles. She is a natural Irish beauty with a dazzling look that requires no makeup or time in front of the mirror. She tailors her own clothes; because they fit her lanky frame perfectly, she always looks impeccably groomed. Even her walk is focused and determined.

Her down-to-earth personality, which makes her a good listener, also makes her a natural for a customer-oriented career such as a hairdresser. Customers like her and tip her generously. She makes customers feel special because she takes great pride in helping them have the right hair style for their type of hair, facial shape, and personality, and she readily communicates these details to them.

Holly's initial financial goal was to continue to live modestly at home with her parents and bring some money home to help with expenses. The arrangement she had at the salon was that she would earn minimum wage and would receive a commission on the portion of the business she generated. Tips were hers. Her strategy was to maintain a lifestyle based only on her minimum wage salary and immediately save what tips and commissions were net after taxes.

She zealously marketed herself and creatively hosted free workshops on Sunday evenings for women's groups in local churches and community organizations as a means of building clientele. She taught them how to select the right cut and style to complement facial features, as well as other points about tinting, painting, and perming techniques. After eighteen months, she had her schedule filled with eight appointments each day—four cuts and styles, two perms, and two tints or paints on average. Her tips averaged 20 percent or more, and she was able to save $250 each week on tips alone. Her goal was to try to save $1,000 a month as a minimum for a six-year period, to give her at least $70,000 working capital to open a salon of her own. She visited my office often so

I could keep her focused on saving and receive periodic feedback on the growth of her savings.

At age twenty-six, Holly had her grand opening.

She has become an entrepreneur in her field, with an established clientele that eagerly followed her. When Holly opened her own salon, she had two other employees working for her. The salon is booked two weeks in advance and is one of the most desirable salons in Fort Worth.

On one occasion of our meeting, Holly stated that she had concerns that her parents did not have enough money put aside for their retirement years. As the oldest daughter, she envisioned herself needing to help support them financially.

As disciplined and focused on her own goals as she was, I remember thinking how remarkable it was for such a young woman to be so concerned about her parents—at a time when her peers are focused on marriage, careers, or beginning families of their own. Holly stated that she felt she would like an insurance policy so that if something happened to her, the proceeds would help benefit her parents and create a small retirement income for them. She chose to put $100 a month into a cash value whole life insurance policy that would provide a $100,000 death benefit to her parents if she died. If she did not die by the time her parents could work no longer, she would borrow from the potential cash values in the whole life policy in the event that her parents needed financial help. Over the years, the cash value insurance could also potentially supplement her retirement income.

At age twenty-eight, Holly married the man of her dreams, Dan, who has similar values regarding money and saving. She continues to save $100 for the purpose of helping her parents, and Holly and Dan have a pact to remain debt free. She and Dan are saving $250 monthly in contributions to mutual funds for retirement. Holly has increased her life insurance to also cover Dan. Dan's insurance program is, likewise, designed to be there for Holly in the event of his death.

Holly's and Dan's financial goals can become reality because they share similar values and are focused on saving rather than debt accumulation.

She states her most recent joy, "My kids will *never* be burdened or have to worry about financially supporting me someday . . . Now let's concentrate on what I need to do to provide benefits to my employees and to invest the profits from my business." Making up for her "short sights" she added, "I just don't know what to do or how to do these things. Let's begin again."

Single Professional Desires to Save

Ann is a thirty-year-old obstetrician who is dedicated to her career and patients. She is a member of a professional firm in Dallas where her practice is thriving. When we first met, Ann told me that during her childhood she "lived a life of luxury," so much so that she felt guilty for her good fortune. It was this sensitivity to others less fortunate that led her to pursue a career in medicine to help mothers and their children.

Ann gave me splendid details of her family estate in Newport, Rhode Island, with its palatial grandeur and flower gardens overlooking the sea. She recalled her great joy at spending summers with her grandparents in Marblehead, Massachusetts. She described fondly that her grandfather taught her all her marlinspike skills so she could tie any sailing or boating knot, and do it "faster and better than any bloke." She laughed when she remembered how her grandfather would let her steady the helm when they were on an easy run sailing out from Cape Ann. She recalls, "He'd tell me that the Cape was named after me, and I believed him of course!" She spent her teen years delivering boats for retiring New Englanders who were relocating to the warmer, bluer waters of the Caribbean. She made the run from the Cape, south through intercoastal waterways to Miami and sailed the final leg to the Bahamas or Virgin Islands.

For Ann, the exhilaration and courage of sailing was in her blood. She missed open water and felt the flat, dry, ranch lands around Dallas to be wanting. She always dreamed of owning a large sail boat like her grandfather's and someday circumnavigating the globe, or at least setting a challenging course that she could accommodate with her schedule.

Since medical school and beginning her practice in Dallas, where her family later moved, Ann truly has had little time—to dream, to sail, or to spend. Her demanding schedule as a physician makes it easy for Ann to focus on saving money. Since our work together, she has committed to save $75,000 annually which is 25 percent of her gross income of $250,000.

Ann is "on a mission" to save for and own a forty-four-foot ketch knowing that a preowned but relatively new craft will cost her about $120,000. As she explains, "Saving for the boat makes the joy and memories of my childhood come alive again. With my hectic schedule, the memories *are* my recreation." She also wishes to accumulate wealth, because in her retirement years, she wants to live a lifestyle without worry as she had as a young girl. She would like to retire at age sixty.

Protecting her assets is very important to her, and she fears a lawsuit but understands that as a physician she is vulnerable in this regard. She is also aware that she needs to be astute to tax planning because of her desirable income.

Needs

If, like Ann, you are newly beginning a professional practice, here are some key issues of concern:

♦ To maximize your disability income protection to help cover personal and business practice expenses in the event you become disabled and qualify for benefits.
♦ To build a short-term emergency reserve of liquid accessible funds before aggressive saving begins.
♦ To maximize malpractice insurance in the event of lawsuit.
♦ To help protect your accumulated savings and assets from exposure to lawsuit.

- To have a short-term savings program to buy a boat or achieve another goal in a few years.
- To build a long-term tax deferred retirement program enabling you to retire at an age that you desire.

Questions to Ask

- What are your present savings that are liquid in the event of an emergency?
- Do you have disability income protection? When does it begin?
- What are your monthly expenses?
- Are you currently contributing to a 401(k), 403(b), SEP-IRA, or profit sharing?
- To date, how much have you been saving on a monthly basis?
- At what age do you wish to retire?
- How much can you save comfortably on a monthly basis?
- Do you presently have mutual funds, stocks, bonds, or annuities?

Ann's Strategy

Ann is committed to aggressively saving 25 percent of her annual income or $75,000. Here is how she diversifies her short-term and long-term savings to satisfy her needs and concerns for the future as well as her goals for saving.

Income Protection

The disability income protection Ann has at her professional firm begins its payout in the event of a covered disability after a 120-day elimination period, at 60 percent of salary to age sixty-five. Also, we put into place an individual disability income policy to reduce the possibility that her income stream for savings could be jeopardized if she becomes disabled and qualifies for benefits. At her age, income level and excellent health, the premium is easily affordable for her.

Short-Term Savings for Emergency

Ann also needs an emergency cash account to cover her personal expenses as well as any expenses associated with her practice if she should become unable to work. (A complete explanation of disability income coverage to protect paying the cost of business overhead expenses is found in Rebecca's story.)

As a single woman without the additional income of a spouse, Ann's emergency fund should be three to six times her monthly expenses. In Ann's case, her monthly expenses were $5,300. She chose to have $32,500 as her goal for liquid savings in a money market account. This type of short-term savings gives her check writing privileges with a checkbook. These funds are available for use at any time without IRS penalties or costly surrender fees.

To create her short-term savings emergency fund, Ann saves $2,700 each month into an interest bearing money market account. She can use it for emergencies if needed or to purchase her boat when the time comes. After the first 12 months, Ann has secured $32,500 in her emergency fund.

Accumulate Short-Term Cash

Ann's other short-term need is to accumulate cash in five years to buy her boat. Ann chooses to invest $32,500 annually into a mutual fund portfolio. After contributing $2,700 each month for about four years, Ann should be ready to purchase her boat if she is fortunate enough to average an assumed 5-percent annual rate of return.

Asset Protection

Ann's fear of lawsuit exposure can be addressed in three ways. The size of her money market short-term emergency fund can help pay for any legal fees she may incur. She has malpractice insurance for the maximum protection allowable. Third, she has a cash value life insurance policy that could potentially provide funds. In Texas, life insurance and annuities are sheltered from exposure to lawsuit. (This is true to varying degrees in many other states as well.)

Ann chose to place $20,000 annually into a cash value life insurance policy. The potential growth of the cash value of the policy may be able to help Ann fund a retirement program. Remember, any potential cash value grows income tax deferred, and the owner can borrow it or *surrender to cost basis* (generally, this means total premiums paid) without income tax if the policy is not a modified endowment. Borrowing requires interest to be paid and will reduce the death benefit. Borrowing will also reduce the cash value and increase the chance that the policy may lapse. But, this may be unimportant for Ann who is primarily concerned about asset protection and supplementing retirement.

Long-Term Retirement

After she buys her boat at age thirty-five, if Ann continues contributions to mutual funds, her cash accumulation in twenty-five years could potentially be about $1.6 million at age sixty, with an average assumed 5-percent annual rate of return without considering fees, charges, or tax implications. However, she knows there is no guarantee of this over the long-term.

Ann's goal of accumulating retirement income can also be achieved by other savings strategies—individual retirement annuity, a 401(k) retirement program or a SEP-IRA. These vehicles are designed for long-term wealth accumulation and are available without penalty only after you reach the age specified by government regulations.

As a group, the professional corporation in which Ann is a principal has elected a SEP-IRA pension plan. They have also chosen to use mutual funds as the investment vehicle. The SEP-IRA contribution also provides her a tax deduction each year.

Ann is young, with potential for marriage and children. So we will need to monitor her progress and wealth accumulation throughout her life stages. Ann diligently reviews her progress twice each year with her team of CPA, attorney, and financial professional. When she came to review her fund values last fall, she was pleased and confident with her progress and liked "being steady at the helm with all the loose ends knotted and tied up." It's been four years since she began her program, and Ann is already checking out the ads in *Yachting* magazine hoping to find the right ketch.

3

To Buy a Home

Single, Striving to Buy a Home, and Protecting Independence

— *Farzana* —

Farzana graduated from Rutgers with a bachelor's degree in business. To most American women, this would be a rather normal expectation. However, for Farzana it was a symbol of liberation—fueled and given life by her mother's own desires. As the eldest born to a couple who emigrated from New Delhi to build a textile business in New York City after World War II, Farzana lived in a closed traditional Pakistani family where women served the home or the greater good of the family. Farzana explained that the endurance of dreams her mother had while "living behind the veil" were fueled by the venerated example of Indira Ghandi; this made it possible for Farzana to think of going to college and the community good that would come after her graduation.

Farzana's beauty was dominated by her gleaming, ebony, waist-length hair, and fig colored eyes. Her hair, which was never pulled back, cascaded over her face as she sat working at her computer. The weight of her hair caused her to walk erect, shoulders back, with great poise. She used a deep earth red lipstick that complemented her olive skin, and she had matching fingernails, so characteristic for New York women. She was striking and exotic. At five feet, eight inches she was as "tall as a bean"; this, she said, was unusual for women of her culture and a trait that raised her status in the eyes of her community. Even her father had to look up to her.

We met in 1990 when I had been in New York on company business. Farzana worked as a manager in an accounting department where a client of mine was vice president. I literally stumbled on Farzana in a private coffee room while she was kneeling on a mat prostrate in prayer. A devout Muslim, Farzana zealously maintained her cultural traditions in what she called, "an awkward corporate world where expressions of religious beliefs were as foreign as a smile." I was later amazed at her discipline to maintain a forty-day fast for Ramadan.

Farzana had worked for thirteen years since college, and at her mother's wishes, was preparing to assist in operating her father's family business. Her father had become seriously ill, and Farzana's brothers were away at college and not able to run the business. Farzana was the one hope for the family. My client invited Farzana to join us for lunch to talk about future planning. At this point in her life, Farzana had accumulated no savings.

I recall Farzana as intense. She explained that her annual income had grown to $75,000 and anticipated that it would remain at that level for the next three years. The majority of her income was taken home to maintain the family and to help with necessary cash flow for her father's wholesale garment business on Seventh Avenue. The increase in synthetic fiber development was competitively eroding her father's textile business, and he chose not to change or modernize. Since Farzana had no savings, I was relieved to find that she had great medical and disability income protection benefits at the company where she worked. These included a comprehensive long-term disability income policy and a 401(k) investment plan, in which she was planning to contribute 10 percent of her income.

After graduating from college, Farzana's steady income had been a blessing to her family and her community. Her deep sense of duty led her to help all that she could. She was supporting her two younger brothers through medical school. Farzana's earnings also supported many bank loans for the family business—loans for which she was ultimately responsible. It had taken $500 per month for the last five years to pay off these loans. Her dream now was to purchase a home for her mother, father, and the family so they could live in the suburbs and move out of their three-bedroom apartment in the "jowls of the city" as she called it. Furthermore, at her income level, the mortgage interest deduction could benefit her when filing her federal income taxes. Farzana was willing to do whatever was necessary on a monthly basis to buy a home in three to five years; then she would be thirty-five years old.

Farzana felt comfortable saving $500 each month because she was accustomed to paying that much on the various loans. She would save an additional $300 that had previously been spent on helping others outside the home. Even though she was earning a good income, Farzana was traditional, conservative, and uncomfortable with financial risk—especially since her income benefited so many.

Farzana was committed to pay cash for family necessities and would cut back on giving money to people outside the family. She knew that if she was going to accomplish her goal to purchase the home, her role and obligation to share the wealth "as the family's financial savior" must change—money lent to outside family members was not considered a loan to be repaid. In fact, the money she gave for children's clothes and medicine for nieces and nephews was considered "a gift" never to be repaid.

Needs

If, like Farzana, you desire to own a home, you need to understand "how much house" you can afford and what relationship that has to your income. You may want to eliminate any possibility that your loved ones might feel responsible to help you if you are in need. Specifically, you need:

- ♦ To save money for a down payment on a house as well as the closing costs. The general rule is that mortgage lenders will require 10 to 20 percent as a down payment. First-time home buyers in many areas of the country can often find financing that is more liberal. Closing costs can vary between 2 percent and 5 percent of the mortgage, depending on locality.
- ♦ To understand every monthly expense in order to determine what mortgage could be supported by monthly income.

◆ To know guidelines for financing. For example, Farzana's $75,000 gross income is $6,250 on a monthly basis; $6,250 x 33 percent equals $2,062. That is the amount that a bank or mortgage company will allow as a guideline for a monthly mortgage payment. Then all debt is added to the above amount. The next rule of thumb is that the total cannot exceed 38 percent of gross income.

◆ To select a price range for houses by calculating the approximate monthly mortgage payment. On an annual basis, your house payments will be approximately 10 percent of the total mortgage, including taxes and interest. For example a $100,000 mortgage will have an annual payment of $10,000. That divided over 12 months would be approximately $833 each month.

◆ To select a well-known local realtor who will assist you in your search and financing.

◆ To help protect your ability to pay the mortgage in the event of disability or death.

Questions to Ask

◆ How much money are you willing and able to save monthly?

◆ Will you have any bonuses or extra income in the future?

◆ Are you willing to take risks with your savings or do you want guaranteed interest rates with no risk attached?

◆ Will you pass the credit report that is part of your future mortgage loan application?

◆ Do you have credit card debt that you need to eliminate?

◆ Is your income protected in the event you become disabled?

◆ Does the bank or mortgage lending company require you to purchase *personal mortgage insurance* (PMI)?

◆ Do you now have, or will you need, additional life insurance to cover the mortgage payoff as well as other needs in the event of your death? (This is known as *individual mortgage protection life insurance.*)

You must understand that PMI insurance is *protection for the bank* or the mortgage lender only. In the event you default on your payments, the bank is protected until they foreclose on the property.

PMI does not pay off the mortgage on your behalf nor does it provide a death benefit to your family in the event of your death.

As a result, many dual-income homeowners elect to protect their ability to make mortgage payments in two ways. Some purchase individual disability income insurance to protect income if they become disabled and qualify for benefits. Some purchase individual mortgage protection life insurance equal to the amount of the outstanding mortgage. There are many ways and names by which companies sell or market this mortgage insurance idea, but it is very important to understand that this is life insurance. Many types of life insurance are used to accomplish paying off the mortgage (for example *decreasing term, level term, yearly renewable term, flexible premium whole life* and *variable life*). Life insurance can also be used creatively to help accelerate the payoff of your mortgage earlier if you live (known as *mortgage acceleration*) or to pay off the bank if you die.

The important distinction between PMI and individual mortgage protection life insurance is that only your individual policy will benefit your beneficiaries in the event that you as breadwinner die before the mortgage is paid. The death benefit your family receives can then be used to satisfy the bank, after which your family receives clear title or deed to the house. After the struggle and sacrifice to buy a home, no one wants to be forced to lose their American Dream.

Farzana's Strategy

To save for a down payment, Farzana wanted guaranteed interest rates without risk, so she selected a credit union savings account with a declared interest rate. She could also have purchased bank certificates of deposit or saved in a short-term money market account. Instead, she chose the payroll deduction benefit of credit union savings. She could not pledge to give away money outside the family if she did not have the money to spend each week when she received her paycheck. She was certain that the credit union approach would ensure regular disciplined savings. For her, it was a matter of honor. With the payroll deduction approach, she truly did not have the money available to give away.

In Farzana's case, her income and debt-free financial status could comfortably support a mortgage, tax and interest payment for a $150,000 mortgage or a $200,000 home.

Because she was the sole support of the mortgage, we determined that it was necessary that Farzana not overextend herself with a mortgage payment that could prevent her from any other long-term retirement savings. As a result, she planned to purchase a less expensive home than she originally planned. She focused on a $150,000 maximum purchase price, because she wanted to keep her house payment around $1,200; she also wanted to begin contributions to her 401(k) retirement plan as soon as possible.

Based on Farzana's income, she began saving $650 each month in a credit union savings for the house. She also opened a money market account into which she deposited $187.50 monthly; after 2 years, she had her short-term emergency fund of $4,500 secured.

Then Farzana saved $187.50 monthly as a 3-percent contribution to her 401(k) plan deducted from her payroll, and the company matched up to 3 percent, for a 6-percent total contribution on an annual basis.

When she bought the home in 1995, Farzana called me to purchase life insurance. Her desire was to provide cash to pay off the mortgage in the event of her death. She designated her mother and father as beneficiaries. Also, several months after her family moved into the home in Fort Lee, Farzana started an investment portfolio with the $650 monthly payment she had been saving to buy the house. Her growing sense of confidence and pride at the accomplishment of purchasing the home for her parents and family, made her more willing to take on a measure of risk.

The day the family moved, Farzana phoned to tell me how her mother sat and cried—outside on the porch—all day. Farzana's voice beamed as she related how the large front room would be left empty for family prayer. The living room had a huge picture window. It faced east.

4

To Accumulate Wealth

Single Professional Woman

— *Mercedes Chandler* —

I knew the moment she walked into my office that this young woman was going places. Mercedes Chandler, who insisted that her compound proper name be used at all times, had a quality about her that commanded attention. She was a five foot, ten inch California beauty—blonde, and tall, built like a model. Raised in Santa Barbara and educated with a law degree from Stanford, her expectations for life were high. I recall a focus and ambition matched only by her sense of confidence. She made it quite clear that "while my brother and sister were squandering Dad's money, partying and drinking on the beach and in the canyons every night of the week, I was determined to make something of the opportunities I was given. After all, what's the sense of coming from wealthy parents if you never have any pride or wealth of your own. I can never go back."

She proceeded to tell me that by age eighteen her brother had become an alcoholic and that her older sister had been in drug rehabilitation for the last eight years. But for all of Mercedes Chandler's confidence, it was sweet to see that she was also humbly grateful for having her undergraduate and law school expenses paid. She declared, "when my parents were going through the stress of raising us, and when John and Amy were living a party life, my agreement with my dad was that if I would stay straight, graduate with honors, and be accepted to law school, he would pay the bills. After all, it was costing him and Mom twice that much for private rehab for the other kids. He agreed."

Mercedes Chandler also proudly recalled that her parents were so pleased with the way "she turned out," that after graduating from law school, they paid for a year off for her to travel through Europe and "buy stuff." She traveled, but saved most of the money.

She was focused and driven. At age twenty-seven, she landed a solid $65,000 job as a personal injury attorney with a firm in Dallas. She wanted to move as far away from California and her "dysfunctional siblings" as possible. Of her salary, she netted $48,000 and was rigorously saving $1,500 a month. Even though she fell short of her goal, she saved $26,000 in her first two years on the job. At age twenty-nine, she purchased a $120,000 condo and came to me to assist with what she called "an aggressive wealth accumulation strategy, so I can become a millionaire on my own like my dad."

Given the curt descriptions about her brother and sister as worthless children, I remember being surprised when she became very serious about her need to marry and raise a family of her own. Mercedes Chandler confessed, "I know I come off as really assertive, and I am great at what I do; however, I do have a soft side that truly wants a family. We were a great family before we grew up. My parents loved each other and loved us so much. I can't stand to see my brother and sister hurt them so much with what they've done with their lives."

Mercedes Chandler was determined to make up for it—and make up for it all. She would be the one her "parents were proud of." She wanted a stable career and "to be established financially before she married."

Needs

Many young women who are children from wealthy families desire to make it on their own. If, like Mercedes Chandler, you are well educated, disciplined, and driven to save at an early age, you'll want to have:

- ♦ Focused, consistent, and diversified savings.
- ♦ Knowledge about benefits available in disability income protection programs.

- Knowledge about ways of protecting your assets from potential liability exposure.
- Knowledge about what's available in the marketplace regarding tax deferred vehicles including life insurance and annuities.
- Knowledge about how to diversify investment vehicles.

Questions to Ask

- Have your parents established a trust fund for you? If so, does it provide a monthly income? When will it be available to you?
- Is there a possibility that you will receive an inheritance?
- Are there any existing family assets in your name such as stocks or bonds?
- To what extent do you expect your income to grow?
- In addition to illness or disability, is your income exposed to any jeopardy relating to your profession?
- What are your monthly expenses and income?
- What are you presently doing to save for retirement?
- What are your balances for mutual funds, stocks and bonds?
- Do you understand all benefits available through your professional firm?
- What is the maximum potential of earnings for your career?
- Do you have an attorney, financial professional, and an accountant working together as you plan for the future?
- Have you organized all of your financial affairs so that, if you died today, your family would know where to find the important papers, whom to call, and how to process your estate?

Mercedes Chandler's Strategy

Mercedes Chandler began working with me when she was thirty years old. She continues to build her public profile by being active in community and church organizations while practicing law.

When Mercedes began her planning, she netted $4,000 income each month. Her mortgage and taxes on her condo were $1,500 monthly, with a budget of $1,000 to cover utilities, car expenses, insurance and any discretionary items she needed. She carried only short-term debt for which she paid the balance within thirty days. I took care to explain that even if she paid each credit card bill every month, it was still a monthly expense that needed to be totaled in her overall discretionary income.

Mercedes Chandler was disciplined and successful at keeping her expenses within the discretionary budget she has reserved because she considered her $1,500 monthly savings a priority. For six months after purchasing her condo, she continued to save the $1,500 monthly to accumulate $9,000 in a money market account for use as a short-term liquid savings fund.

Her employee benefits also included a great disability income program designed specifically for her needs. It carried an "own occupation" provision which means if she became disabled and no longer able to practice in court, but she was able to teach school, her policy would still pay her the benefit as long as she qualified.

Her basic life insurance protection needs had been satisfied with three times her annual salary (which has since grown to $100,000) or $300,000 of term insurance through her professional firm. Her intent was that this will be more than enough to satisfy the mortgage on her condo in the event of her death.

When we reviewed her future goals and desires, Mercedes Chandler claimed that she also hoped to marry an attorney someday and to begin their own family practice together. For this reason, she became concerned when she realized that the $300,000 of term insurance she had with her firm would not be portable in the event she left the firm. She was also keenly aware that her age and excellent health were in her favor. As a result, she chose to apply for an individual cash value life insurance policy, which included a waiver of premium option; in the event she was disabled and qualified for benefits, the premium contributions would be paid. The insurance would provide her tax deferred potential cash value growth. The potential cash value could also help her fund future expenses such as college tuition or provide her with a retirement benefit.

Mercedes Chandler and I took time to organize her portfolio of benefits available through the firm, as well as her personal investment portfolio and life insurance statements. She maintains a close look at her portfolio binder and keeps focused on her quarterly profits and losses.

At age thirty, Mercedes Chandler was feeling the peer pressure of her colleagues whom she characterized as "heavy into the purchase of luxury cars and the like." I will always remember her response, "I guess my financial values are very different. I don't buy seasonal fashions or short-term luxury items that depreciate. I'm more oriented toward the long term and like when my purchases appreciate rather than depreciate like a car the moment you drive it out of the car dealership."

Mercedes Chandler has her own drive to create financial stability and aggressive long-term savings for accumulation. With or without a man, she is well on her way to her American Dream of becoming a millionaire in her own right by age fifty—if not much sooner.

5

To Raise a Family

—— Jeanne ——

Jeanne was referred to me in 1990 to begin retirement planning. She intently told me her life story and how she came to her current financial situation.

Jeanne and Dan were married on May 5, 1973. She was a beautiful bride in a traditional white gown, and Dan was handsome beyond belief in his black tuxedo. She was careful to provide me with each and every detail of their wedding day—something that was as vivid as if it were yesterday. Jeanne told me about how gala the reception was with plenty of food and guests dancing under the moon as the band played on and on.

Jeanne mentioned that there was nothing unusual about their marriage. They were a typical American dual-income family, and they loved and respected each other. Their first son, Craig, was born in 1975, and Amy was born shortly thereafter. Jeanne was quick to point out that she and Dan both shared the household chores and raised the children. He loved the kids and wanted to be active in their lives—even with "all the little things." Dan was always protective of Jeanne. She said he "wore" his arm around her waist; she was five feet, one inch; he stood at five feet, ten. Weekends were spent having picnics and family gatherings. They lived for their family, and Monday morning usually meant going back to work so the bills could be paid.

In 1984, Dan was thirty-four years old when, as he and Craig were coming home from karate lessons, Dan experienced an aneurysm on the brain. Jeanne's world came to a halt. While Dan was in intensive care, the doctors doubted that he would live. Then, if he were to live, the question was to what extent he would have brain damage. The VA hospital had a coma center, and Jeanne wanted desperately for Dan's case to be on the waiting list so that someday he could be placed in the coma unit. After many weeks, Dan was moved to the VA hospital at Jeanne's relentless insistence.

At the time of Dan's seizure, his care at the VA was without cost to Jeanne. (This is not the case today.) During this time, Jeanne started to pull together her disability and life insurance policies along with becoming knowledgeable about Dan's benefits at work. She applied for Social Security six months after Dan's aneurysm, and later she started to receive the income for Craig and Amy along with a Social Security check for Dan.

Jeanne worked for the telephone company and was a member of the union when Dan became hospitalized. She had a boss who was compassionate, caring, and understanding. He encouraged her to take care of herself and the children and to work whatever hours she was able.

After some time, the VA hospital declared that because Dan's aneurysm was not caused by war, he must move out and into a nursing home. Jeanne was overwhelmed with having to care for the children, financially support the family, and carry on with life. Not being able to share her feelings with her love and confidant incapacitated her. She could not talk, think, or be responsible without him actively involved in her life.

The VA hospital helped her find a nursing home that was equipped to handle Dan's extreme and special needs. The VA also paid for the first six months of Dan's nursing home care. (The government benefits no longer provide this.) After six months, Jeanne needed to turn over Dan's Social Security check and the disability benefits that Dan received from his employer to the nursing home to pay for his care. Jeanne not only had lost her best friend and husband, but she also lost his income to help support their home and children.

Jeanne relayed to me the stress she had as she drove home one evening after a full day at work. She was ready to give up and to just continue driving. Thoughts of her children needing her and memories of happy times with Dan flashed before her. She knew she was ready to face the future.

Seventeen years after their wedding day and six years after his aneurysm, Dan died in 1990. Jeanne supported the family by working herself up the corporate ladder into a management position with the potential of higher earnings. When her employees experienced family problems, the impact of her own experience enabled Jeanne to show the compassion that was once given to her by her former boss.

When Jeanne began to work with me in 1990, we invested the money received from Dan's insurance, and she began saving in her 401(k) plan at work for retirement. She purchased life insurance for her and her children. She attended all the school functions for Craig and Amy. Her focus was to be both mom and dad to her children and to take them on some great vacations throughout Texas to visit relatives. Craig is now in his fourth year of college and is studying sports fitness. His Social Security check stopped when he graduated from high school. Amy is a senior in high school and looking forward to college and accomplishing her dreams of becoming a physical therapist. Her Social Security check will stop too. There was a time when government assistance would have continued to help the children through four years of college.

Jeanne needed to support herself and her family for a long time. She received no Social Security for herself, but was thankful her children had some help after losing their father. Jeanne has accepted life for what it is, and when she prays, she remembers the good times and looks forward to the years ahead. She is aggressively saving for retirement—but only after the bills are paid.

Before Dan's accident, Dan was persuaded by another agent to cash in their insurance. The agent believed that there was no benefit to such cash value life insurance and that it was "inferior as an investment." Dan and Jeanne cashed in their $150,000 cash value life insurance policy in August 1982. It was replaced with a $100,000 decreasing term insurance policy—there was no waiver of premium placed on the new policy, which would have paid the premiums during the six years Dan was disabled. Furthermore, Jeanne was paying for a policy that was eventually worth much less than the amount originally purchased. A split-second decision to surrender cash value life insurance cost Jeanne more than $60,000 when Dan died. Dan was convinced that "buy term, invest the difference" was a great decision. Jeanne learned otherwise.

Protecting a Special Needs Child:

At age fifty, Ellen was an industrious and studious woman whose caring and sincerity were contagious. Ellen, who worked at building her career in the banking industry, waited until age thirty-five to marry. Her husband, Frank, had been previously married with children of his own. He was an attentive and financially responsible father. He had teenage sons and a younger daughter for whom he assiduously provided the best of everything. The boys excelled in football and gymnastics. His daughter was an Olympic caliber swimmer and hoped to someday become a concert pianist. He assisted his children's mother financially at every request. He was very proud of his children and he intensely continued a supportive relationship with them after his divorce from their mother.

Ellen longed for the day she and Frank would have a child together. When Frank learned that their son would be born with Downs syndrome, it created great emotional stress for him. Moreover, his ex-wife continuously expressed her financial concerns. After Johnny's first birthday, Frank explained that the additional responsibilities were too great and much more than he had anticipated in a second marriage. Ellen and Frank separated, and Ellen was realistic enough not to expect that Frank would return.

Ellen had lived the next thirteen years totally absorbed with caring for Johnny, who she considered to be "the total center and joy of her life." She received much happiness from watching him grow and had a heartfelt joy in the innocence and gentleness he would find in all that he saw and learned every day. The grandparents had a great love for Johnny whose smile was immense as he gave them a "big bear hug."

During our meeting, Ellen expressed concerns about what would happen to Johnny if she died first. Frank's heart and financial responsibilities were with the children of his first marriage, and he was mailing only sporadic financial support for Johnny at birthdays and the holidays. Ellen was resigned to this for she knew realistically that Frank truly was not financially capable of providing more, and she did not choose to pursue it and cause added stress in her life. She believed that, "going it alone was definitely the easier alternative."

Needs

If you have a special needs child, your concerns are overwhelming. Like Ellen, you need to make arrangements for your child's long-term care in the event of your death. Perhaps, you also need to explore options with halfway housing. Priority needs include the following.

- ♦ To have trust arrangements made for the child.
- ♦ To have a disability income program.
- ♦ To have life insurance and know who is named beneficiary.
- ♦ To know the value of your pension and who is named as beneficiary.
- ♦ To know what any potential inheritance will be.

Questions to Ask

- ♦ Have any legal trust arrangements been made for your child?
- ♦ What is the value of your pension?
- ♦ How much life insurance do you need to take care of special need concerns?
- ♦ What is the value of your parents' estate?
- ♦ Do your parents have a long-term care policy?
- ♦ Have your parents made arrangements for the transfer of their assets by means of wills or trusts?

Ellen's Strategy

Ellen has a $750,000 life insurance policy with benefit proceeds intended for Johnny's care. She named her parents as beneficiaries when she purchased the policy ten years ago; then her parents were younger, and she felt they were capable of taking care of Johnny in the event of her death.

Ellen has worked in a corporate setting for years and has a $75,000 income and a superior benefit program. Her son is on her medical insurance program. Not knowing the future, this provides reassurance for Ellen. Johnny also receives a monthly Social Security check. Ellen has always used this for his special needs such as paying for a nanny if necessary. Ellen's pension has accumulated to $350,000, and her parents are named as beneficiaries.

Her home, which she purchased when she was twenty-nine, was paid off last year; her parents' home was paid off as well. The value of Ellen's home is $150,000 and the value of her parents' home is $100,000, and there is a large parcel of land valued at $200,000. Her parents have set up their wills and trusts leaving all to Ellen.

For the sake of argument, if Ellen and her parents died in a car accident while traveling to pick up Johnny at school tomorrow, the total value of both estates, including Ellen's life insurance for Johnny, is valued at $1,675,000.

Ellen is thankful and proud that her father has his planning in order. However, Ellen wants to remove the stress and burden of Johnny's care from her aging parents. Ellen needs to meet with her attorney to structure a trust where she can direct her assets and remove her parents as beneficiary on all of her accounts. Based on Ellen's desires, her attorney can guide her about what type of trust to establish.

Ellen needs to have an organized written folder with her financial papers and policies in order in the event that she dies, and she needs to discuss her finances with her parents so they can understand what will happen to Johnny. There are several hypothetical situations that could occur.

- ♦ If Ellen predeceases Johnny, she needs a legal trust that will specify living arrangements and care for him as long as he lives.
- ♦ If Ellen predeceases Johnny, and Johnny dies soon after, Ellen needs to also specify in the trust that the balance of her assets will protect her parents until they die.
- ♦ Both her parents' and Ellen's legal trusts should be handled in tandem. Doing this will help ensure that in the event Ellen and her parents die before Johnny, provisions will exist for his care. They also need to specify how to distribute the balance of funds, if any, in the event of Johnny's death.

As her financial professional, I will join her CPA and her attorney to continue to monitor Ellen's investment and insurance needs throughout the years.

The comfort of working with a professional team gave Ellen the confidence she needed. She was genuinely proud, thankful, and confident that Johnny's needs were provided for even if both she and her parents were not there to see him smile or give him his favorite "big bear hug."

Married Woman Raising a Family

— Angela —

Angela and Vinnie are upper middle class, second-generation Italian-Americans in their early 40s. They were high school sweethearts and are still married after twenty years. Vinnie is a salt-of-the-earth type, loving father, and "family man." His fun consists of playing a round of golf in a league each week, and he enjoys Dallas Cowboys football. Occasionally, there are late night poker games or bets in the football pool. Angela works as a loan officer in a prestigious bank, and Vinnie is a pilot with a well-known airline. They have two daughters; one is in college, and the other is in elementary school. Angela has a disability program as a benefit through the bank. Vinnie is also covered through the airline.

Together, they have a combined income of $125,000 and are underinsured considering that they hold a mortgage of $90,000 plus the responsibility of college education for two children. They are both contributing 10 percent to their 401(k) plans, and they understand very well the performance of the various funds. As a banker, Angela monitors their 401(k) plan performance and is astute to how the market is performing.

When Angela was referred to my office, she was stressed and exhausted—emotionally and financially. I remember her panic, "We are doing everything we can. The pressures to achieve it all are just too much. We are overwhelmed at times. As a parent, you wonder if it will come together. I'm here, because I'm afraid that we just can't do it all. We have many expenses now, another child to enter college in ten years, and we just don't know how to juggle everything and still save for retirement."

Angela and Vinnie are "on track," but they both are looking forward to the day when the girls' college educations are paid. They want to build a dream home in the South, but don't think it will ever be possible. Angela is concerned with her high-stress position and its long hours. Expenses are high due to the needs and desires of a growing family. Because Vinnie works with the airline and the family can fly free, they have grown accustomed to the expectation of taking several costly family vacations abroad each year. Angela's business responsibilities keep her wardrobe expenses high. Their daughters are Olympic hopefuls; therefore, gymnastic expenses are high, and there are music lessons, a third car for one daughter away at college and the college phone bills! All create a situation where their attractive dual-income is totally exhausted each month. Expenses equal net income.

Needs

Parents of dual-income families raising children have pressures that they cannot easily contain. If, like Angela and Vinnie, you and your loved one are working hard and are torn in many directions—pulled by career, household expenses and chores—life may not be fun.

The years when you should be enjoying your children rapidly pass with little quality time for the family. Providing taxi service and car pooling for children's activities sever critical family time together. Families are eating out more. Weekends bring even more stress to have fun. Family time is again diminished by errands that cannot be done during the week—laundry, dry cleaning, grocery shopping, mowing the lawn, gardening, painting, decorating, entertaining, and shopping until you drop. The cycle is often vicious, and all you want to do is stop the train and get off!

There is even less time for long-term saving, which is often viewed as "something you'll do later when you can afford it." It is seen as another burden rather than as a structured way to achieve financial success. Each year when you file your taxes you cringe and ask "where did it all go?" You often have nothing to show for your hard work! These critical years of growing a family bring significant responsibilities. During these years, you can't afford not to plan. Here are common needs among dual-income families:

- ◆ Each spouse needs to consider maximizing disability income coverage to help protect the mortgage payments, monthly expenses, and contributions to insurance and investments in the event he or she becomes disabled and qualifies for benefits.
- ◆ Each spouse needs to consider life insurance protection on the other in an amount that can cover the mortgage expenses as well as help replace lost income.
- ◆ With a college student driving eighty-five miles one way each weekend, the family will need personal excess liability protection in the event that she is in an auto accident with coeds or anyone else.
- ◆ They need to continue to save for the education of the second child who will be entering college in ten years.

Questions to Ask

- ◆ Do you have any debt?
- ◆ What are your monthly expenses?
- ◆ What is your combined gross and net income?

- ◆ Is your job secure?
- ◆ Do you have a short-term emergency savings or money market account?
- ◆ Do you and your spouse have income protection?
- ◆ How much life insurance are you carrying on each other?
- ◆ Do you have a will?
- ◆ What is the present value in each spouse's retirement account, and are you maximizing contributions, and attaining optimum growth?
- ◆ Is your auto insurance liability protection adequate for teenage drivers?
- ◆ Will you receive an inheritance?

Vinnie's and Angela's Strategy

Vinnie and Angela can boost their peace of mind considerably by first helping insure that their protection needs are met in the event that either becomes disabled or dies—which is a high risk for Vinnie given his occupation as a pilot. The fact that the family is financially overextended demonstrates that the family lifestyle cannot be sustained if either income is jeopardized due to disability or death. In America, the realities and necessities of the dual-income family have put an end to the old myth that women do not need to have life insurance. Any dual-income family would be hard pressed, even with a male head of household, to retain its standard of living if the woman's income suddenly was not available due to death or disability.

Vinnie and Angela need to increase their life insurance on each other. Vinnie has $250,000 of life insurance, but his $90,000 income qualifies him for $900,000. Angela has $70,000 term insurance at work. Her $35,000 income should qualify her for $350,000. Vinnie should apply for $650,000 and Angela should apply for $280,000. It should be diversified using both term and permanent insurance based on a fact-find and cash flow analysis. Both Vinnie and Angela are fortunate to have disability income protection at work.

Beyond their current 401(k) contributions, it is unrealistic for this couple to believe they can do more. However, they can take charge of reducing their financial stress by focusing on monthly expenses and working at creating a new lifestyle with fewer expectations. Perhaps they can consider fewer vacations even though their airfare is paid. Each family member can't have it all. Together as a family they should discuss the financial facts of life and agree on limiting the added luxuries that become financial burdens as well.

I find that lifestyle issues are often the easiest for a family to resolve together as a team. Here are a few ideas my clients from dual-income families have shared as ways of simplifying life and cutting expenses:

- Assign times to do the household chores and errands—as a team; with everyone working, chores can get done quickly.
- Attempt to set aside some time during the week for the family to be together.
- Encourage teens to earn spending money to support their entertainment.
- Create a community youth exchange where the neighborhood kids do errands for other families. Often it increases their sense of self-esteem and responsibility to work for someone else. Teach children and teens how to write checks and have a checking account. Teach children early that money comes as a result of working—not from a plastic card placed in the cash machine at the bank.
- Exercise your right as an American raising a strong healthy family to leave work at a reasonable hour. A steady habit of working late nights and weekends without other days off will not keep a family together.
- Eat out less.
- Limit student after-school activities to one day a week rather than four or five. Get students focused on doing a few things very well rather than have the whole family scattered and running wild to keep up with the Joneses—who are also running wild.
- When they are in junior high school, begin to encourage students to learn about available college scholarships. By having a sports, an academic, or an art scholarship as a goal, students will have a specialized focus for their after-school activities rather than having no direction until it's too late. Take advan-

tage of your school tax dollars and consult your high school guidance counselor about scholarships.

I also encouraged Angela and Vinnie to meet with me along with their CPA and attorney to help the family through these tough years. Their attorney needs to create or update a will. The fact that their professional team will meet with them together will give an enormous sense of self-confidence for Angela and Vinnie. They will know that they are not struggling alone without support. After the second daughter graduates from college, Angela and Vinnie can begin aggressive savings for retirement and their dream home.

6

To Divorce and Remarry with Children

Divorced Parent Starting Over

— *Dee* —

The number of american women who are single parents and heads of households grows each year. My divorced women clients share intensely personal and riveting stories. Divorced parents seem to have the most complicated set of factors at play in their efforts to put themselves on a solid course. They are uncertain about being able to save wealth for the future. They are dealing with their own economic and career influences, as well as the tenuous economic circumstances of an ex-spouse.

   Issues of trust, loyalty, fear of failure, fear of "doing it all alone," not to mention anger, can all arise to make divorced parents vulnerable, anxious, and confused during the months following divorce. My clients who are divorced parents with growing children tell me they are so exhausted and overwhelmed about the present, that they cannot even begin to think about the future. They recall anxiety over parents, friends, and attorneys telling them what to do during the "rejection and divorce war." After divorce, many women claim that they are emotionally shattered, fearful, and incapable of making decisions on their own. Yet, divorced women feel a strong desire to be affirmed and to feel "fulfilled, attractive, and loved," which are feelings often coupled with a deep need to have a daily "father figure" in their children's lives. In a few years, life can become even more complicated and difficult when either a divorced father or mother contemplates remarriage. What I have witnessed in my practice is that the second marriage often cannot survive the emotional, financial, and legal stress. Ultimately, more than half of second and third marriages fail.

Women who have gone through the experience offer these insights.

"I was totally blindsided and ill prepared to be alone and face all the nurturing and financial responsibilities of my children. There was so much I didn't know—legally and financially. There should have been a seminar or course out there to teach me what not to do and what to do. I probably would have stuck it out in my first marriage and definitely not remarried. I was in such shell shock from the first divorce that I was hopeful that a second relationship would be a help."

—SEE

"I think every woman who contemplates marriage owes it to herself to understand everything there is to know about the financial ramifications and legal issues involved with divorce. Once there are children in a marriage, the financial consequences and uncertainties of a divorce can set you back to square one. Actually, it's worse than starting over, because after divorce, you're older and everything is harder."

—MK

"I had three kids; the guy I was dating had two. I felt we shared a common bond. Perhaps I remarried because I felt that it would be easier if we were both raising our kids together . . . I was thinking of myself and my children and was totally unprepared for the realities associated with his ex-wife and her demands on him on behalf of her own children. Any single mother thinking about remarrying should take time to investigate all financial issues so she can be aware. Believe me, if you thought the end of the first marriage was no fairy tale, the second marriage can offer double jeopardy, especially if he has children of his own."

—MJS

"My friends had cautioned me about rebound relationships after I was divorced. I was devastated, lonely, and in need. But I did take the time to rediscover myself and to become more responsible. I was open to the possibility that I was also to blame in my failed marriage and took time to realize how I may have contributed to its demise. I joined a health club, became active in my church, and concentrated on quality time with the children. It took years, but I was satisfied that when I met my second husband I was mature, strong, and confident about what I had achieved on my own with my children. I was ready and whole to begin again."

—EJ

"I went through the ringer during my divorce, and I was determined to never let it happen to me again. Three years ago, I thought I had fallen in love and actually was planning to remarry. My best friend, who was a single parent and who was divorced twice, took me aside and strongly suggested that I take some time to totally analyze the situation. I met with my attorney and agent, and we spent time working out various scenarios for the future regarding my children, my parents, and my retirement. It was the best thing I could have ever done. I realized that the understanding and common values that I thought I had with my future husband were all in my mind. When I started talking about a prenuptial agreement to protect my inheritance and assets, he was uncooperative and used mind games about "having no faith in our future together." I basically said that a prenuptial agreement encouraged open communication. When it came down to it, he never showed up. The hard dose of reality was really worth the effort because I diverted another disaster. The biggest lesson I learned was that it is *my* responsibility to plan and to provide a strategy for the future—no one else's. I ended up feeling much better and more confident about my own strength to take care of my children and my future. I may have been emotionally hurt again, but I avoided being hurt financially as well."

—ASK

Dee was thirty-four years old and working as an executive secretary. She was proud of the opportunities she created for herself and readily admitted that with a $40,000 salary, many Americans coming from a small town would consider her successful for achieving such a salary without a college degree.

Dee was ambitious. She was a dark Mediterranean beauty with long brunette hair. She had been a social butterfly; she eventually married Brian, her high school sweetheart who had been captain of the football team.

Both were gregarious and popular; people told them they'd go far with their "good looks" and "great personalities." Brian attended a prominent university north of Milwaukee and became an engineer. Dee's front office poise and presence made her perfect for dealing with the public, and she easily obtained a position as a receptionist at the corporate office of a large local dairy and cheese product manufacturer in Wisconsin.

Dee was eager to move the marriage forward and to begin a family; many of her friends were enjoying pregnancy and motherhood. Brian, however, was just becoming established at the engineering firm, and he was not yet financially secure to begin a family; he wanted to pay off his student loans. Dee was convincing that she could work part-time, be a mom, and work within a budget. They had two sons within two years of Brian's graduation.

Dee told me her story. "I remember that I liked kids when I was growing up, and we had a few of our own because I felt as a woman it was the thing to do at that time in my life. I was a cheerleader; Brian played football; we were king and queen of the prom. When we were married, we looked like the little couple on top of the wedding cake. The exhilaration, attention, and prominence Brian and I both had in high school just ended. He went on to college and grew as an individual; but my life just seemed to stop. All the happy high school times quickly became past memories as we started to fight over finances and whose responsibility it was to take out the trash as we were tripping over blocks and toys. Brian was devoted, loyal, and a great father, but I wanted more. I blamed my own unhappiness on him. I thought he was responsible for making me happy. My attitude was childish. Brian just couldn't put up with it any more. He had this conservative image of how his mother and father ran a household—home cooked meals every night, home sewn clothes, a neat house to come home to, and his shirt freshly pressed each morning—everything I didn't do."

Dee and Brian both worked. Brian wanted to save and be responsible financially. Dee was unaware and unconcerned about the household finances and thought that her part-time job justified increased spending. She wasn't responsible and didn't accept the fact that she spent much more than what they both earned. They had different values about what was important in those early years.

Dee paid for the extras: designer clothing, European cosmetics, boutique decor for the house, and nightly dinners out. Brian paid for the mortgage, cars, household expenses, insurance, savings, and retirement.

The divorce was a struggle similar to what most couples face, but Dee was satisfied with the settlement. Her friends and family encouraged her to get the house. Dee was leery to pay for the upkeep on her own. Instead, her attorney negotiated for Brian to pay health care and to educate both sons through college. Dee "had realized too late how important it is for a husband and wife to share similar values about finances if a marriage is to grow and thrive." She also learned how valuable continued education was if she was to achieve higher earning potential.

Needs

If you are like Dee, and during your marriage you were not financially responsible, divorce probably means that you are starting over with a new commitment to be responsible in ways you may not have been in the past. If you have children, you will need:

+ To obtain life insurance protection on each parent for the benefit of the children in the event that either parent dies.
+ To obtain medical coverage for the children.
+ To create a short-term savings fund that also provides cash flow in the event that child support payments are irregular.
+ To select a professional team and begin serious planning.
+ To analyze all expenses relative to net monthly income.
+ To protect the income stream of both parents in the event of disability.

Questions to Ask

+ Do you have disability income protection coverage?
+ What are your total monthly expenses?
+ What is your net monthly income?
+ Will you receive child support on a regular basis and how much will it be?
+ Is your ex-spouse responsible to carry out the financial obligation of monthly support payments on an uninterrupted basis?
+ Who is responsible for providing medical insurance coverage for the children?
+ Does the ex-spouse carry life insurance? Who is designated as the beneficiary?
+ Do you have life insurance?
+ Do you and your ex-spouse have separate wills?
+ Do you receive additional financial help from others in your family?
+ What type of benefits do you have at work?
+ Do you expect to inherit any money in the next five to ten years?

Dee's and Brian's Strategy

Brian's retirement remained intact after the divorce. Therefore, at age thirty-four, Dee did not have a home, or any individual retirement program of her own except what she would receive from Social Security. Her divorce settlement also gave her the second car, which was older, but paid off. She requested half of the 401(k) retirement, but instead, her attorney suggested Brian pay her $10,000 to be used as an emergency fund.

Dee realized too late the costs of not being financially responsible. She committed to becoming responsible and being involved in her own retirement and financial future. She is looking forward to the day when she will be able to begin her own plan because the dairy company where she currently is employed has no retirement program.

Dee's children, Terry and Troy, were ages fourteen and twelve at the time of her divorce. They are relying on her for emotional and financial security. She knows that they are growing up in

Brian's footsteps with a love of football, sports, and their dad. They resent being away from him.

After the divorce, Dee was pressured by her family to buy a small house of her own; they thought the mortgage interest deduction would be a significant benefit to her when filing her tax return. But Dee was afraid of the added responsibility, expenses, and unforeseen maintenance associated with owning a home. She met with her accountant to review the financials associated with owning vs. renting. Tax benefits of owning a home were not considerable enough for her. In relationship to the tax benefits, Dee's increased expenses and purchases associated with buying a home would be an encumbrance, and she would have no emergency savings if she used the $10,000 from her divorce settlement to purchase a home. Dee was resolved. She simplified her life and rented a town house to avoid such worries.

Instead, the $10,000 that Dee received was placed into a conservative mutual fund account; $6,000 was placed in a money market account for use as an emergency fund, and $4,000 was placed in a growth fund. The $6,000 money market account has a checkbook and is earning interest.

Dee then needed to address her $40,000 salary and how she could stretch her monthly net pay to cover rent, utilities, food, clothing and all the extras to which she had been accustomed and the extras for growing boys.

Dee needed to provide for income protection needs. In the event that he dies, Brian is carrying a life insurance policy to provide for child support until their sons are twenty-one and to cover the commitment for college. The divorce settlement provides for each son to attend a state college of his choice.

She applied for a personal disability income policy for $2,380 a month. She felt secure in knowing that if she became disabled and qualified for benefits, the policy would help her pay the bills and the groceries.

Dee also applied for a $400,000 term life insurance policy. Some day, she hopes to convert it to a cash value insurance to supplement her retirement, but due to her income, she is pleased with the amount of coverage she can purchase inexpensively.

She has met with the attorney to update her will and put a life insurance trust in order to help secure the children's support if she should die. By having a life insurance trust, she can designate how the money is to be used by those who would care for her sons in the event that she dies. She does not want to name Brian as beneficiary on the policy even though she knows if she dies he will have custody rights. With the help of her attorney, she can set the terms and guidelines for use of the life insurance proceeds within the trust. If Dee dies, the trust receives $400,000. If it averaged an assumed 5-percent annual rate of return, the trust should be able to provide $20,000 annually for the housing and support of the boys in the event that the children are minors and the father dies.

Dee expects to receive an inheritance of approximately $150,000 when her parents and elderly aunt die. Her aunt is her godmother and has no one else to whom she can bequeath her estate.

Possibility of Remarriage

Two years after her divorce, Dee became financially concerned about the impact of a prospective remarriage in her life. Dee had always thrived on the attention that men gave her; she said it made her feel good, and she liked it when men were "nice to her." But nice is not enough. A divorced parent contemplating remarriage must approach any future relationship like a business. Dee was tired of being without a man in her life and vulnerable. It was hard for her to wipe the stars out of her eyes.

Dee needed to protect her personal assets. She needed to begin a discussion to determine her beau's income, his child support payments for his own children, as well as his total debt. She also was determined to talk to other divorced parents who had entered second marriages.

If Dee truly wants a long-term relationship, the total financial picture for both partners must be explained by each of them—not just verbally but—in black and white with both accountants present. It should be a time to review life insurance, and disability income protection policies, W2 statements, and retirement account statements. This is the time to ask questions as if your future depends upon it—because it does.

Questions to Ask

+ Do you each know the other's total financial status in terms of assets, gross and net income, and expenses?
+ How much debt are you both bringing to the marriage?
+ What is the extent of both parties' work benefits?
+ Where do you each fall in the priority order of legal responsibilities to your own children and your own ex-spouses?
+ What are the "unspoken or unwritten or informal" emotional, legal, financial, or other responsibilities each of you has made to your own children and to your own ex-spouse on their behalf? For instance: what are the monthly hidden costs beyond child support such as music, dance, or gymnastics lessons; recitals; musical instrument purchases; first car and insurance; exchange student opportunities; summer camps; other travel opportunities; vacations with friends; etc.?
+ How do the unspoken commitments to ex-spouses and ex-grandparents impact the hierarchy of time, attention, and finances you can give to one another in this new emotional and financial relationship?
+ Will you need to move into new housing to accommodate all the kids for vacations, weekends, and holidays?
+ Does distance from step children of both families create other financial or time factors that can have a strong impact on your new family unit?
+ If something happens to either in the remarriage, how do you want insurance proceeds to be addressed?
+ What is the duration of child support—in terms of what is to be received and what is to be paid to another ex-spouse?
+ If one of you becomes disabled, how is income and child support affected?
+ If you are unable to work, his child support payments to his children are his first priority according to law. Will he also be able to support your joint living expenses together as a family when your full pay check is not there? (This is the 30 to 40 percent of your income that is uncovered by disability income insurance.)

◆ Will you both agree to a prenuptial agreement drafted by your attorneys?

◆ Do you know the child support and custody laws in the state or county that governs where the other's divorce decree was granted?

◆ According to applicable law, does the income you add to the joint family you create positively affect his "ability to pay" regarding additional demands by his ex-spouse on behalf of his children as they grow and the cost of living increases?

◆ Can you both afford life insurance with each other as the beneficiary, in addition to the policies that you each have for the benefit of your own children?

◆ Ultimately, do you both share the same values regarding raising children and finances?

Dee's Strategy

Dee and her beau can wait to remarry until their children are grown and on their own. In the meantime, they can find emotional support during romantic weekends alone. This could prove to be the least stressful financial alternative.

If Dee chooses to remarry while the kids are growing, she needs to first understand the financial and legal parameters and discuss a prenuptial agreement with her beau and attorney. Each needs to reveal total finances to each other, so if either dies, the surviving spouse is not left to deal with the other's ex-spouse. Each needs to define long-term goals.

Her beau needs to commit to a life insurance policy at ten to fifteen times his annual salary and name her as beneficiary. He needs to have a disability policy to cover his income.

He and she both must have properly written wills and trusts for the benefit of both sets of children and for the benefit of each other.

Dee's children's education is promised. But her beau also has obligations to his children. If he is responsible for them, he needs to put money aside to accumulate the approximate estimated cost of a state college education in ten years according to College Board tables.

If Dee's ex-husband, Brian, is responsible for a similar amount for her children, Dee needs to ensure that money is being set aside for the children's education.

Dee needs to ensure that she will not cosign any loans for her beau's children in addition to the financial commitments she has to her own. In the event of a second divorce, if her beau is unable to pay a college loan that Dee cosigned, the bank holds Dee responsible to pay the loan—regardless of what the legal divorce settlement stipulates.

As a newly remarried couple, Dee and her beau both must agree on how to save, for what purpose, how much, and who is paying for what! They must agree to keep their retirement funding separate. In the event the second marriage doesn't survive, their individual retirement savings will not be jeopardized; no one will be forced to make a lump sum payment in the event of a second divorce. The days are over when retirement accounts are considered applicable to only the husband in the household without any separate emphasis placed on the wife's retirement needs.

Both people in this remarriage have experienced the issues, the heartache, and the betrayal of divorce. From this point forward, they both should agree on open dialogue and insist that there will be no hidden agendas with ex-spouses. Each should consider that all debt as well as promised inheritances or savings belong to him and his children or her and her children. Secure this in a prenuptial agreement or other legal planning recommended by an attorney prior to remarriage. All future decisions about investments, home, and retirement should be determined together by Dee and her new husband.

With all of their baggage checked, the couple should be ready to embark on a new journey.

7

To Care for Aging Parents

Single with Aged Parents

Pam

Pam, a smiling brunette who loves inland fishing, is in her mid-forties and secure in a nursing career. She had been the department head in a large teaching hospital. In 1992, she sold her ranch in El Paso to take a new position on the Gulf Coast in Corpus Christie, Texas, near her father and mother, who are in their late seventies.

Pam has taken on a role as caregiver for her parents; however, her parents have not been totally open with her about their wishes and plans for the future. Pam does not know the details of their life insurance program: how much they have, what company it is with, or how the beneficiaries are assigned. She has concerns about her parents becoming ill and whether she would need to consider nursing home or in-home care. She has heard her friends discuss concerns about the administrative fees associated with probate, and as a result, Pam wonders whether or not her parents have a current will.

When Pam was introduced to me, she was concerned about this new milestone in her life when she began worrying about her aging parents. Pam has a brother who is ten years her senior, but she knows that because of his own lifestyle, business commitments, and lack of closeness, he would share little if any participation in their elder parents' welfare—emotionally or financially. Matters were made worse when her brother told her that their mom and dad put $77,000 cash in little cigar boxes hidden under the floor boards of the linen closet. Both parents had deep memories of the Depression and recall the fears of their parents losing money when the banks closed.

Pam was confused about what to do first. She mentioned, "The worst part of all, is that as a family we never discussed these things with our parents. There was always silence when it came to issues such as money, death, and the future. Because there was no common discussion about this when we were growing up, we just can't discuss it comfortably now." Pam had no idea what to do or what it was going to take for her parents to be responsible to communicate with her. Ultimately, it would be Pam who would be faced with their financial decisions in the future, and she was in a position of responsibility but had no idea of their net worth. Her father was a retired coal miner from Pennsylvania who moved to Texas in the late 1970s because of his health. He had received a monetary payment because of his black lung disease.

Needs

If you have aging parents and find your situation similar to Pam's, you need to initiate discussion to uncover the facts. Parents who have experienced the Depression have deep feelings about their financial struggles and losses from that time. But they must understand that if their financial affairs are not in order and communicated to their children, the children could pay large legal fees and estate taxes, not to mention the time and frustration of getting matters in order after the parents are deceased. The irony for the family will be that lack of planning could cost what the parents have hidden and saved under the floor boards in their cigar boxes. Consider the following approach:

- ♦ Gather any pension statements and life insurance policies and understand their provisions to ensure that beneficiary assignments are up-to-date.
- ♦ Be introduced to and begin to work with your parents' attorney and financial professional.
- ♦ Understand the medical coverage and any outstanding medical bills that have accumulated with their illness.
- ♦ Investigate the local costs for *custodial care* at a nursing home and/ or in-home care.

- Work with an attorney to establish a *statutory power of attorney* to enable you to run the finances and monthly bills for your parents.
- Work with an attorney and your parents' physicians to establish a *health care power of attorney* to aid in making health care decisions for your parents in the event you are unable to do so.
- Work with an attorney to determine if your parents' will is current.
- Work with an attorney to establish a *living will* for your parents that includes their directives regarding whether they want to be kept alive by artificial means.
- Work with your parents to determine their wishes regarding burial or cremation services when they die. Join them in making final arrangements to put these affairs in order at an appropriate time.

Questions to Ask

- If parents are on a fixed income, is there a shortfall in monthly income to cover increases in prescription expenses or medical expenses not covered by insurance?
- What are the provisions and how are the beneficiaries assigned on parent's life insurance policies, bank accounts etc.?
- In whose name are bank accounts, certificates of deposit, stocks, bonds, or mutual funds listed?
- If the family estate is valued at more than the current maximum for federal-estate-tax-free inheritance, have there been provisions made to create a trust or otherwise provide cash to address the federal estate tax potential?
- If your parents have elected custodial care, how will it affect the assignment of their assets? To the children? Or to the nursing home?
- If your parents face financial jeopardy, what portion of your discretionary income is available to assist them?

Pam's Strategy

I suggested that the attorney, Pam, and I meet together with her parents. I encouraged Pam to openly discuss her concerns. Having the attorney and I there made it easier for the issues to be discussed openly.

I analyzed the insurance policies and created a summary that explained each policy, contract numbers, company of issue, death benefit amounts and beneficiary designations.

I recommended long-term care coverage with an in-home provision for each parent. There were many types of policies for Pam to review. Many provided for nursing home care, others provided both in-home health care and nursing home care. The parents selected an appropriate plan based on their feelings.

The attorney reviewed the will and informed them that the will was outdated. It had not been reviewed since Pam was a little girl, and it had another family member who was deceased listed as a trustee. The attorney informed her parents that it was common practice to have *statutory power of attorney* documents drawn. The power of attorney would enable Pam to write checks, pay bills and make other financial decisions on their behalf if either parent should become incapacitated. An updated will was written. The attorney also suggested that her parents notify Pam of the location of their bank accounts, stock certificates, and other financial papers; he had requested a summary of all accounts to organize all records. He would then review these and recommend actions to simplify matters for probate reasons. Having organized and properly assigned accounts prior to the death of each parent would minimize probate fees after the death of each.

Pam also brought her own insurance policies to the meeting for review. She was concerned whether she needed to provide financial help to her parents, her own disability income coverage and life insurance were properly designed if her parents would be relying on this income. Pam originally had her brother listed as the beneficiary of her insurance. She had genuine concerns that if she predeceased her parents and her brother received the death benefit, he would not necessarily share her same wishes to use the money to take care of their aging parents. The attorney suggested that Pam designate a trustee, because he recommended that her insurance be placed inside of a trust in order to secure the care of her parents if Pam predeceased them.

Even though Pam's parents would always consider Pam as their "little girl," I made them understand that a time would come when they may not be able to handle their own affairs. Her father was a proud man who had a hard time dealing with the fact that his daughter would someday be taking care of him. I communicated to her parents that the most important issue they needed to decide was whether they wanted the IRS and nursing home to potentially receive their assets or whether they wanted to leave a legacy to their son and daughter.

8

To Own a Business

Starting a Business

— *Rebecca* —

"I've spent fifteen years working for other people whom I felt had lower standards than mine in this business." That was the first assertion I remember Rebecca making when we met. She was thirty-seven years old and had "had enough of working for others."

I cannot forget how passionately Rebecca voiced her convictions when she exclaimed, "Doing what I love should not make me feel this miserable! I want to be in control of my destiny. I want to be as creative as I want and manage my daily hours according to the priorities that I set—rather than according to what someone else thinks I should be doing. And when my customer is happy, when my intentions are noble, when my work is excellent—it is fun. When I excel at what I love, this is my happiness. This is my measure of success."

Rebecca stated what other women believe in their hearts each day they go to work. She echoed the passions and beliefs that I hear again and again from many women who have launched private enterprises.

To say that Rebecca was driven and determined was an understatement. This woman was full of energy, and failure was not an option. Her fire was fueled by the realities of raising a daughter on her own after a very bitter divorce. She claims her dedication and long hours at work with a well-known public relations firm was "a strain on a marriage that just wasn't strong enough to survive a wife and mother working long hours outside the home."

Rebecca wanted a total overhaul of her life. Instead of retreating in self-doubt, she moved forward into even higher risk and uncertainty by starting her own business. She was attractive, creative, intellectual, sharp, and outspoken. Rebecca stated that she had been "through the muck of it and down on herself;" she wanted to shed twenty pounds that she attributed to stress and lack of appropriate exercise. Rebecca was a no-nonsense, sturdy, hardworking woman and a salt-of-the-earth type on whom everyone could depend to accomplish the impossible at the last hour.

Rebecca will face many issues and concerns throughout the life cycle of her business.

General Needs During the Life Cycle of a Business

The life cycle of a business begins with the pride, motivation, and desire to start a venture that will succeed through various stages during its growth and development. The following concepts are what Rebecca learned during our association; her knowledge of what to expect built her confidence about her new venture.

For a moment, let's have you join Rebecca for an overview of Business 101.

Coordinating a Professional Team

I cannot encourage you enough to take the time to select and develop trusting relationships with a banker, CPA, attorney, and/or financial professional as your professional team. Take the time to communicate with them quarterly. It is their input in the early months of starting your business that can give you the expertise and emotional support you need. That you receive education and attentiveness from every member of your professional team is absolutely essential. If months go by and you feel that one person just doesn't have the time to communicate with or teach you what you need to know, it's time for a change. Many women believe that unless they can communicate their concerns openly with a professional, they wouldn't be encouraged to develop a relationship where they can learn what they need to prosper.

Banker or Loan Officer

Your banker or loan officer will provide you a sample *business plan* to show you what is necessary in order to obtain financing. Establishing a business plan and learning how to predict business cycles and expenses is one of the primary fundamentals for a beginning entrepreneur who intends to market expertise and talent. There are many books on the market to assist you in developing a credible business plan.

Your banker or loan officer will then evaluate the loan potential of your business based on additional input from your accountant and the attorney. There are different types of loans the bank will consider. First is setting up a line of credit. A $50,000 *line of credit* requires that you complete a financial statement based on past record. The bank reviews the earnings power of the new business and will set the interest rate and payment conditions. A line of credit loan is designed to help only if you are in need of supplementing cash flow based on expenses. This type of loan is generally used for a young professional who will possibly need back-up financing in the early start-up months of the business.

A second type of loan, *a lump sum loan*, is often needed for the down payment or outright purchase of a business or building. The bank may be looking at business potential, book value, profit and loss. Collateral is often required for a lump sum loan; because of this, any cash value life insurance policy you have can be considered toward your collateral. The bank will also request term life insurance on the owners in order to be protected in the event of death of a loan holder. (This is known as a *collateral assignment* where your business pays the premium for a policy for the specific amount of the loan, and the bank is named as beneficiary as long as there is an outstanding loan balance for the amount owed.) The bank retains the policy and should return it to the owners after the debt has been paid.

Certified Public Accountant

Your CPA will assist you in understanding the various types of business structures and how they impact taxation. Sole proprietorships, partnerships, S-corporations, and C-corporations all vary. Use your CPA to help you decide what structure is best for you.

On an ongoing basis, your CPA will also help you stay focused on your profit and loss to monitor growth of your business. If you should later decide to sell the business, the CPA will determine its financial worth by providing a market analysis for the value of the building as well as your profit and loss over a period of time, usually three to five years.

Attorney

Early legal concerns for a start-up business involve purchasing and leasing agreements that must be drafted or reviewed by an attorney. The attorney will be concerned with all legal aspects of the business and will be your advocate regarding all clauses in your contracts.

Your attorney also is responsible for incorporation. The attorney assists you in establishing *bylaws* that are a key legal provision when establishing a new corporation; the bylaws establish rules to govern the internal affairs and regulations of your organization. If the building, leasing arrangements, business or professional practice is comprised of more than one individual, bylaws must be drafted and put in order. Bylaws are designed for the protection of everyone who is responsible for the growth of the business or who has signed their name to the purchase of the building or leasing commitment. The bylaws will require many conditions.

Financial Professional

The financial professional whom you select for your professional team should have expertise in business insurance planning and recommend other financial professionals who can provide liability and medical plans. Your primary financial professional should educate you about how to use insurance to help protect the business and your employees.

Protecting the Business

Liability insurance will be needed for the building and the business. It is designed to protect the building in the event of fire, theft or other catastrophe such as on-premises injury. Additional types of *errors or omissions insurance* or *personal excess liability* coverage can often be purchased to help safeguard against liability and exposure due to professional or technical performance of duties by you or your employees.

A new business that operates with more that one partner often purchases key man or *key person insurance*. This is for owners, partners, or other contracted employees. This life insurance is for the purpose of paying the business a sum of money that would equate to the value of the person's contribution or expertise in operating the business. If the key person is responsible for one-third of the debt and cash flow to the business, then for the business to survive, it needs to be reassured that cash will be available in the event of the death of this person. The life insurance proceeds help in the replacement cost of hiring new talent to fill the loss.

The owners of the business often purchase *disability overhead expense* coverage to help cover business expenses. The purpose is to cover employee wages, utilities, outstanding loans, taxes, professional fees, and other monthly expenses. Subject to certain policy limitations, the policy will generally cover all expenses of a business except supplies. The insurance company will determine if it will insure the owners and the amount it is willing to insure depending on the nature of the occupation and the extent of expenses. The owner/s must be healthy and insurable without a major medical condition at the time of applying for the coverage. All members of the group will need this type of coverage to help insure that the mortgage payment and business expenses are covered in the event that one of the members becomes disabled and qualifies for benefits. For example, if there are three owners, and the expenses for the business are $6,000 per month, the program will provide that each owner has coverage for $2,000. This protects each owner and generally is a requirement for a bank loan.

The owner of a business corporation also can set up a formal *wage continuation* arrangement. As an employer, you need to set guidelines for yourself and for employees about how anyone would get paid in the event of a disability. If you *do not have* a formal wage continuation arrangement adopted as a resolution, any paycheck you receive if you become disabled may be considered an ad hoc dividend payment that is not deductible to the business. The IRS will allow a formal wage continuation arrangement drawn by your attorney to have parameters. For example, the owner will receive 100 percent of income for the first ninety days and then the disability policy will pay to age sixty-five if the owner becomes disabled and qualifies for benefits. The terms should be written and formally be part of the company resolutions prior to your disability.

There are many ways to use *business owned life insurance* to help the future success of a corporation if the principal owner dies. The corporation pays the premium and is beneficiary. The business owner is the insured. If the insured dies, the insurance company will pay the benefit to the business helping it to continue at a time when the business could have severe cash flow problems without the owner. This is similar to key person insurance. Your financial professional can help you determine the best type of policy for your business.

Protecting the Employees

Beyond establishing initial coverage to protect the key person and building, the continuing cycle of business development involves employee benefits. The following *group insurance* benefits are discussed in sequence according to order of importance for the employees and according to availability of cash flow of the growing business. These are the ones most commonly used by many small businesses.

Group health insurance comes in many forms and is available to as few as one employee including the owner, depending on the state. First, you determine what you want in the form of benefits and company rating. Health insurance can be purchased to cover costs associated with *medical, maternity, prescription, dental, vision, and preventative care.*

Long-Term Retirement Plans

A variety of pension and retirement benefits are available for you to provide to employees. These include 401(k) plans, profit sharing plans, deferred compensation, and executive bonuses. Often it is the retirement plan that helps your business to attract and to retain top notch talent.

A *401(k) plan* is commonly used in settings of ten or more employees. It allows employees to create a retirement plan by payroll deduction from their salary on a pretax basis. The amount is determined by the overall census and incomes. An employee can individually pick the investments for contributions based on risk tolerance generally with a family of funds. If you are interested in pursuing a 401(k) plan for your business, you'll need to seek a pension administrator and a financial professional.

In addition to providing disciplined savings, the 401(k) plan can be taken with the employee if no longer employed at your business. Upon leaving the company, the employee has the right to transfer the vested fund amount into an IRA or the new empoyer's company-sponsored plan. Also, if any 401(k) or profit sharing plan is canceled due to lack of employee participation, the employer and employees retain their vested fund amounts and can transfer the amounts into IRA accounts, which they will personally own and monitor.

With *profit sharing* plans you, the employer, contribute to the plan on behalf of each employee as well as yourself as long as you are an employee. Generally, the employer contributes to this plan and the employees do not. Up to certain limits, you as the employer decide each year how much or how little to contribute. The benefit to the business owner is that if you are an employee you can contribute on your own behalf as well as your employees', and the money you contribute is tax deductible to the business.

As a business owner there are other retirement programs that can help provide retirement funds for you and your employees. *Deferred compensation* and *executive bonus* programs are among these. Your financial professional can explain these to you and help you determine the program that's best for your situation.

Business Continuation

Eventually, you will retire. *Succession planning* will help you look for someone to continue the business that you began. To understand the options available and details to address when creating an arrangement, you need to meet with your financial professional, attorney and CPA together as a team. (See Megan's, Boots's, and Anita's stories.)

A *buy-sell agreement* is a contract in which the business or the owners agree to purchase the business interest upon death, disability, or some other occurrence of one of the owners. You enter into an agreement that is designed to protect the value of the business for the principals involved

A *buy-sell disability arrangement* is also available. These contracts can be designed to have a lump sum payout or monthly income determined by the amount to which each of your partners and you agree. The contracts and insurance policies will address how "total disability" is defined and you qualify for benefits under the terms of the policy.

As your business grows, it is imperative that your professional team proactively communicate with you and among themselves. It is imperative that the financial professional, CPA, and attorney each have expertise and experience in business issues—preferably with first-hand experience from running a business of their own. You want a team that's knowledgeable to advise you about pensions, benefits, legal issues, tax issues, and succession planning issues—everything involved in the life of your business.

Now that you have a broad understanding of key issues involved in establishing a business, let's return to Rebecca and see how she began. She was on a mission. From now on she would have her business, her rules, her profits, her headaches, and her losses.

Needs

If, like Rebecca, you are talented and motivated with the drive and ambition to begin your own business, here are critical items you should consider. You need:

♦ To determine if you will begin your enterprise alone, with a partner and/or with a staff of employees.

♦ To consult with business planning professionals to create a complete three-year business plan that considers all expenses, income, and staffing contingencies.

♦ To have adequate start-up capital to sustain your personal living expenses as well as business expenses for three years.

♦ To interview and select a CPA, financial professional, and attorney that suit your style and to develop working relationships with them. Preferably, you should seek professionals willing to take the time to teach you about what needs to be done and the reasons why. In order to ensure that your team can relate to your concerns for the start-up business, you would probably select a professional team from among those who operate their own businesses with support staff. Associates who practice with large conglomerates often have not personally experienced the concerns of the sole proprietor or partnership.

♦ To select an appropriate site location and negotiate the lease. Have an attorney draft a contract for lease or purchase that is favorable to your needs, or have your attorney review the contract which is presented.

♦ To determine a suitable location that allows for future growth.

♦ To protect a partnership or corporation in the event of disability or death of the principals.

♦ To protect your income stream and cash flow as a sole proprietor in the event that you become disabled and qualify for benefits.

♦ To hire associates with expertise who will share your vision for the company.

♦ To help minimize employee turnover by retaining associates with a benefit package.

Questions to Ask

- ♦ Do you have a professional team in place whom you trust and who will teach you as your business grows?
- ♦ Will you need additional funding to run the business?
- ♦ What do you foresee your receivables to be on a monthly basis? Can you predict seasonal cycles for your business throughout the year?
- ♦ What was your last annual income prior to beginning your business?
- ♦ What are your personal monthly expenses?
- ♦ What does your business plan estimate your monthly business overhead expenses to be?
- ♦ How much life insurance do you have and who is beneficiary?
- ♦ Do you have a personal disability income protection policy?

Rebecca's Strategy

As confident as Rebecca was about her own skills, she was also keen enough to know that as a creative whiz she needed help with administrative skills and front-office expertise. She elected to begin her business as a partnership with a colleague. They agreed to "try it out together for five years."

Financing

Rebecca put a business plan in order because she had a long-time desire to open her own advertising agency and public relations consulting business. She felt confident with her technical skills, but she was concerned about what to do financially to run a business. While she was with her previous employer, she established a $50,000 line of credit. She had many satisfied clients who committed to keep their advertising services with her if she opened an agency of her own and hired staff to execute the work.

Rebecca used a $150,000 certificate of deposit that she received as an inheritance as collateral for her business loan and found a building to rent. She also made her shopping list for office equipment, computers, and necessary materials to start the business.

Selecting a Professional Team

Rather than both partners using a variety of people, Rebecca and her partner chose to work with one professional team in order to simplify and coordinate all matters.

They had the attorney draw up a buy-sell contract assigning their individual value in the business to be $250,000. They each applied for $250,000 of insurance. If either were to die, the insurance company would pay $250,000 to their business, and the business would in-turn buy out the interest of the deceased partner.

I also advised Rebecca to have her attorney review the leasing contract. After review, Rebecca had the leasing company change the contract to include a disability clause that would allow her to end a five-year lease in three months if she was considered to be totally disabled and could no longer operate the business.

Rebecca was also encouraged to meet with her attorney regarding her personal planning; these additional discussions considered updating her will. She needed to communicate her thoughts about what would happen to her daughter if Rebecca were to die. Rebecca named her brother as executor of the estate, and her will designated the $250,000 death benefit to pay for her daughter's care.

Both Rebecca and her partner each applied for a disability income protection policy. The insurance company reviewed their income for the previous two years and determined a benefit amount based on the promise of the business and their past work performance. Rebecca also requested a purchase option rider on the policy to allow her to increase (without showing additional evidence of insurability) the amount of benefit, within limits, as her income increases.

Overhead expense disability income protection was also purchased for the business. The insurance company issued this coverage based on the business plan expenses and financial statement provided to the bank. If a bank loans a new business money, most likely the insurance company will issue an overhead expense policy assuming she meets medical requirements. Rebecca found that requirements vary among companies. With two partners in the business, and $12,000 in monthly expenses (not counting their income or supplies), each partner purchased an overhead expense policy to provide $6,000 per month to the business in the event that either became disabled and qualified for benefits.

After reviewing the business plan, we spent a great deal of time helping Rebecca and her partner become aware of how important it is to stay focused on cash flow and expenses. Their short-term goal was to accelerate cash flow and to monitor profit and loss. They learned how to draw a salary from the business as personal income. To do this, their first focus was to have enough receivables from continuous projects. They developed a three-payment system that initiated receivables upon signing each job contract rather than waiting for projects to be completed and delivered before receiving payment.

Providing Benefits for Employees

Rebecca was excited about her new venture and wanted to consider offering a benefit package for herself, partner, and two employees. She chose a health insurance program after requiring three quotes. She limited the benefits to health insurance at the start, and offered an above-average, hourly wage to attract and keep employees and to compensate for not being able to provide a full benefit package because of cost. She was cautious with a start-up business.

As the business grows and the profit and loss statement indicates an increase in profits, Rebecca and her partner can begin to consider more employee benefits. A future benefit package can include payroll deduction life insurance, group disability income protection coverage, and a 401(k) or other pension plan.

Rebecca also needed to stay focused on her own personal retirement planning. She was busy and overwhelmed with beginning the new business, but that made it all the more necessary to stay focused on her personal long-term goals. It was her personal retirement planning goal as well as planning for her daughter's education in eight years that assisted her in determining how much business profits needed to grow.

Rebecca and her partner had planned to reevaluate their association after a five-year period. At that time, Rebecca called to tell me that the partnership was dissolving, but it was for the better for both of them. When the partnership dissolved, the beneficiaries on all the insurance policies were changed and reassigned to personal family members.

Rebecca was proceeding on track. The partner was "going back" to work for someone else's profit.

Retiring Business Owner

— *Megan* —

Megan was single and sixty-two years old when we met for the first time. All her life she had idolized her father and studied "to be just like him." She and her brother were from a happy-go-lucky Irish-American family who loved life and dancing. Her older brother married the daughter of a department store owner; he went to work with her father and was molded to take over the business. That left Megan with a choice to help in her father's family business. It was a challenge that she accepted with great zeal and success. She followed in his footsteps and became a CPA in Las Colinas, Texas, where she also employed two women. She never imagined that life would speed by so quickly. She had so much fun and loved doing what she did that she just "never had the time to get married."

Megan spent a great deal of time telling me about her needs and desires. She wanted to retire in three years, at age sixty-five, and devote her life to working with youth groups at local churches. She knew that she needed to find another partner who could work side-by-side with her daily to gain knowledge about her clients. Hopefully, she would also purchase Megan's business.

Megan found a young, eager woman, Lisa, who appreciated the opportunity to learn from Megan. Because Megan had built her business through long-term relationships with her father's most trusted clients, she felt a pride and deep sense of responsibility to ensure that the clients were comfortable with her successor. The three years they would work together would provide Megan with the confidence that Lisa was the right choice for the clients.

Megan's attorney and personal CPA worked on the value of the business and put an arrangement in place that would allow Lisa to receive minimal income while learning from Megan. When Megan retired, Megan would continue to work two days a week to help with the continuity of the business for a year. Megan would also be available on a consulting basis to Lisa for a maximum of five years.

The business was to pay $3,000 monthly income to Megan for two years, and a $1,500 monthly income for the next three years. This arrangement was made instead of a lump sum buyout because Lisa did not have the financial resources nor did she feel comfortable with carrying the large debt. Megan wanted the arrangement to succeed for her, Lisa, and the clients; so, she adjusted her retirement lifestyle based on the buyout arrangements.

Megan recalls, "After the initial planning, the time melted away quickly. It seemed to come overnight." She began receiving her individual pension and Social Security benefits as well as receiving the income from the business as agreed in the succession arrangement. Megan's household expenses were little because she had paid off her mortgage while she was working. She also retired without debt.

Needs

If, like Megan, you are a business owner facing retirement, you should consider the following:

♦ To have your attorney draft a formal succession arrangement stating: 1) terms, 2) conditions, 3) amount, and 4) duration of the monthly income you will receive from the business.

♦ To have your accountant determine the value of the business in order to ensure that the purchase price the buyer is offering is realistic.

♦ To understand Social Security benefits and when to apply for them.

♦ If a pension plan had been funded throughout your active working business career, you need to determine its dollar amount so that you can have those figures to calculate the monthly income.

♦ A successor for the business will need to have in place a disability program that can help ensure you of your monthly income in the event she becomes disabled and qualifies for benefits.

♦ The successor also needs to have a life insurance policy in place (with you named as beneficiary) for the value of the business in the event of her death.

Questions to Ask

♦ When do you wish to retire?
♦ Do you want to sell the business outright?
♦ Do you want to have a lump sum buyout or a one- to five-year buyout program?
♦ How much money do you think your business is currently worth?
♦ What type of monthly payment is realistic?
♦ Do you have a retirement account, and what is it worth?
♦ What are your personal monthly household expenses?
♦ What are your retirement goals (travel, purchase retirement home, etc.)?
♦ Do you have life insurance? What is the value of the death benefit? Who is beneficiary?

Megan's Strategy

Megan planned well. Being debt-free allowed her flexibility in the way she sold and transferred her practice to a successor. Had she carried a large debt load, it may have been more difficult to accept the five-year buyout arrangement she made with Lisa.

She needed Lisa to have a disability income protection policy on herself as well as a disability income overhead expense policy for the business. This would help protect Megan's monthly buyout payment over the five-year period in the event that Lisa became disabled and qualified for benefits. This was reassuring for both women because if Lisa became disabled, the practice could remain open and Megan's promissory note could also be protected.

Lisa also applied for a $126,000 term life insurance policy to protect the total amount of the buy-out value of the business in the event of her death. Megan was named beneficiary on the policy.

In the event that Megan could no longer work, she kept her own disability policy in force for the first year of the business arrangement. This would help Lisa replace Megan's services that were promised two days a week.

Megan also had a $75,000 cash value life insurance policy that protected her earlier mortgage that was now paid off. Megan remembers how her brother questioned her about purchasing a cash value life insurance policy to cover the period of her mortgage; he was advocating that she purchase a term policy instead. She remembers her conviction to choose cash value insurance over the term. Now that the mortgage is paid, Megan is ecstatic to learn that the cash value life insurance has proven itself because the policy is worth more than the initial $75,000. She has changed the beneficiary and assigned the proceeds to her church.

A decision to purchase cash value insurance that was considered by her brother to be "foolhardy" many years ago today enables Megan to leave a proud legacy to support church youth programs. Even without children of her own, Megan's heartfelt wishes to make an impact will be felt long after her death.

— *Boots* —

"By being both a physician and a teacher, you can provide the greatest gifts to humanity . . . I always considered teaching as the one profession that I hold higher than being a practicing physician. And I enjoyed teaching at a coed university. Don Meredith, who was a student at Southern Methodist University, was an all-American football player. The coach said that his team would be better players if they took modern dance, and Don was in my modern dance class. There he was, that clown, that wonderful person, going through the motions of modern dance—all influenced by a teacher. Teachers influence people to greatness . . . That's how I got from Texas to the Women's Medical College in Philadelphia—through the direction of a teacher later in my life, after I had my bachelor's and master's degrees and had been teaching.

"I often wonder when someone goes to medical school at age twenty-two, or enters any profession without having real people experience, if that doesn't contribute to their "mightier-than-thou" desire to direct someone's life . . . It's been a different relationship for me with patients. I realized that I was a person long before I became a physician and that patients are people. You must first listen and address the humanness and concerns of people through teaching."

Dr. Boots Cooper believed that a teaching process was integral for all women to learn about health, finances, and parenting. She believed women should demand that professionals "teach them" with the sincerity, caring, and patience of the best teacher they remember. Boots demanded that of herself as a physician helping people with their medical needs; she demanded it of me helping her with her financial needs.

I was in my agency one day when the office supervisor came to me and said that a woman physician, the "much respected Dr. Boots Cooper," called requesting help regarding her insurance program and overall planning. She asked that a woman return the call, preferably a woman who conducts her business by teaching—Boots didn't understand how financial programs and insurance worked.

She didn't want someone who would just sell her a product but someone who would come out to see her and teach her. I called Boots and reassured her that I would explain all that I could.

On the appointment, I found a lady whom I instantly loved. Wearing her white lab coat, she appeared to be a small-framed women and wore her gray hair short and stylish. Her staff was happy and cheerful. Her office was pleasant, nonmedicinal, and comfortable. I saw an ashtray on her credenza, and I wondered if she smoked; there were no ashes.

As a physician, Boots had a $50,000 life insurance policy, and I explained what her policy would do for her. She had some cash value built up in the policy, and she had taken a small loan on the policy to purchase medical equipment. Her coverage was fine, and as we proceeded to discuss her needs and desires for the future, she could determine if she wanted to add to it. Through our interview, Boots said she wasn't sure if she needed the policy because she was not married and had no children of her own. In the event of her death, she wanted to give a tax-free benefit to her nurse who had been loyal for so many years. We completed the forms to assign the nurse as beneficiary.

I inquired if Boots had a disability income program, and she indicated that she needed help in this area because she hadn't done good planning. Proceeding with the fact-find, we diagnosed that her practice had good receivables, but that what she took home was minimal. It didn't take long to realize that Boots had devoted her life to children and had given a great deal to the Girl Scouts of America. Much of her monthly income went to children whom she took in off the street because they needed a home.

She said it was a tough road to become a cardiologist, and her real love was helping other women become successful. I asked her what she meant by success. She defined it as "being happy doing what you're doing." As a teacher in her own right, Boots had an impact. As a physician, she spent her life teaching children and women that success comes from achieving inward happiness and from bringing happiness to others by helping them—rather than from material consumer wealth.

Boots recalled that another agent had called on her a year earlier and recommended that she use the dividends in her life insurance policy to buy more insurance. The agent didn't take the time to understand her values and concerns, and she had no intention to do further business with that agent. After that, Boots called my office searching for a "teacher" to solve her needs.

Boots and I researched what she needed for disability. When we had all the information about her personal and monthly business overhead expenses, my next question was to ask her if she smoked. She smiled and said she had three cigarettes a day—in private. We laughed because I smoked, too.

Because Boots was in her mid-fifties, I was also concerned about business succession planning for her medical practice and asked if she had any plans for someone else coming into the business if anything happened to her or for someone taking over the practice so she could retire. Boots looked at me, smiled and said she thought about it but hadn't done anything. It would be a future need.

We worked out a disability income protection program. Boots's ability to afford it wasn't an issue. How much insurance she could obtain was. Her business expenses were $6,000 each month, in addition to her personal expenses. However, she had no debt.

The following week, we reviewed the disability application and further discussed her life and desires. She explained that she was called Boots because she grew up on a farm and always wore boots and jeans. As an accomplished and highly educated woman, her humility was astonishing; she truly preferred that everyone call her Boots.

We developed a great relationship. She would keep me updated, and I'd continue to encourage her to consider beginning a succession arrangement for her practice. We also discussed how she could leave a continuing legacy for charitable institutions through the gift of life insurance.

One day I received a call from her nurse saying that Boots had become ill and wasn't feeling well. Boots and I met, and she insisted that she would be okay. She was thrilled that the disability income program could help take care of her in the event that she couldn't work and qualified for benefits; the office would continue to run; the home bills could be paid. I continued to ask if she gave any more thought to bringing someone else into the business.

After a few months, Boots's health further deteriorated, and it was necessary for her to go on disability. It was hard for her because it meant backing down from her practice. Other doctors helped her, but no one could be found to take over.

One day she called and said she didn't have much time. She wanted me to review the $50,000 life insurance policy because she would like to give the benefit to the Girl Scouts of America. I told her it was a noble gesture.

She thanked me for my help and said she just wanted to say how important it was to her that I took the time to teach her. She said, "Being a physician I have always made it my practice to teach rather than just do. I gained patients with that approach over the years because patients seemed to understand the process of what I was doing for them." She said I did the same for her and insisted that women "never lose vision of requiring that they be taught." I was overwhelmed that this wonderful, humble lady, who was dying, was taking time to thank me.

After Boots's death, I kept involved. In her will, she gave her home to her nurse to enjoy the back yard with its magnolia trees, creek, and bird feeders. She had given to everyone. The terminal benefit on her disability policy was considered by the nurses to be the greatest gift of all because it paid one extra month after her death. The policy was in force five years before Boots became disabled. The $18,000 premium paid over that time enabled the business to run and personal expenses to be paid for nineteen months. She received $9,000 each month for a total of more than $170,000 in benefits before she died.

I continue to provide service to the nurse. Developing our relationship means that the nurse calls me as her life changes. We get together again and again and continue to grow. We were still concerned about the future of the practice. The hospital made arrangements for another doctor to take it over. The successor had a different bedside manner, and this arrangement did not succeed.

Boots is gone, but her legacy is great. There was never a question of letting her down in any way. She called. I was available. She needed me. I was there. She fulfilled every dream and helped many women. Overall, her influence reemphasized that as women we need and want to be taught. We want to go through a methodical process of learning. At each step, we want to understand what we are doing. We don't purchase without first acknowledging the emotional concerns that motivate us. Only then it is right for us. As a great teacher, that was Boots's greatest lesson of all.

9

To Manage Wealth

Karen

Karen was holding her infant daughter, Amy, in her arms the first time I met her. The baby was surrounded by toys and joy. Karen's husband, Juan, looked on with pride.

Karen is tall, with beautiful shoulder-length, chestnut hair. When she speaks, she speaks with compassion and confidence. Her laughter and smile are sincere. She is the type of woman everyone would want as a best friend. Juan is a tall, dark, and handsome physician who is driven to succeed.

Karen and Juan were new to Texas where Juan had recently started his neurosurgery practice. His first concern was to have a good disability income insurance program in place because he understood the need to protect his income stream. He wanted an *own occupation* disability program which would pay a monthly benefit if he could not perform surgery. (In Juan's case, *own occupation* means if he sustained injury to hands, eyes, legs, or back and could not perform as a surgeon, but he could teach, consult or perform patient care only, he would receive his disability income check, plus his earnings from his other work.)

As we conducted a thorough fact-find about his personal and professional holdings, Juan explained that he wanted disability protection and proper life insurance for him and for Karen. I remember thinking how progressive he was because I did not have many male clients who readily understood the need for having separate life insurance protection on their wives. Juan explained that he had given Karen full authority in choosing what benefits and investments she felt were right for them based on their needs and goals. He also explained that he wanted an aggressive savings program that would enable him to accumulate wealth to an extent that he had the personal choice of when he wanted to retire in the future. He asked that Karen and I inform him when we accomplished the first $1 million savings toward his personal goal of $5 million.

As Karen and I reviewed their insurance needs and ability to pay, I took the time to explain and teach her how different products worked, and she in turn went home and explained the ideas to Juan.

Juan and Karen agreed that their first objective was to put the disability income and life insurance in place. The love they had for each other and their daughter was evident. Their first goal was achieved by a noncancelable individual disability income protection policy with an own occupation definition as he had requested. They also chose a non-cancelable disability income overhead expense policy that would help pay the office bills in the event he became disabled and qualified for benefits. Cash value life insurance was also their choice. It provided tax deferred (and, in Texas, creditor protected) potential for accumulation of cash to potentially supplement Amy's college education, or a supplement for retirement.

It was clear that they intended to be serious and disciplined and would eventually accomplish additional goals that would provide for their long-term needs and desires.

Coordination among the Professional Support Team

Our next step was coordinating a team of professional support so that Juan could practice medicine, and Karen could stay focused on the financial needs of the business and personal financial growth. Their team consisted of CPA, attorney, practice management advisors, pension administrator, and me as the financial professional.

The attorney ensured that proper trust documents were written and in order, then she communicated with me so that we could make arrangements for the cash value life insurance to be placed inside of the trust.

The accountant informed me of the corporate year-end salaries of the physician and employees. I supplied information to their practice management team and pension administrator. The pension administrator prepared all documents for Juan's business profit sharing plan along with year-end statements and sent these to me. These values enabled me to inform Juan and his employees about the values in their retirement plans. The practice management team and my staff stay in close communication regarding health insurance, disability income insurance, and pension funding because the practice management team pays all bills and keeps ongoing records for the medical practice.

Karen had done what Juan has asked of her—to watch over their financial affairs. She proactively kept in contact with each professional; each gave her updated information quarterly. Karen focused on the cash flow of the medical practice, funding their insurance protection, and saving aggressively in mutual funds, stocks, and bonds to achieve their personal wealth accumulation goals. She was committed to and supportive of Juan's desire to reduce employee turnover by providing them superior benefits. Several years ago, she was able to tell Juan that he had accumulated his first $1 million of wealth. He responded with a smile, and it was obvious that he respected her abilities and her keen sense about money matters.

Karen is a woman to be greatly admired because she demanded to be taught about all legal, accounting, financial, and operations matters from the start. As things turned out, these skills and her planning were even more important than she had initially imagined.

During the subsequent years, she learned that life is full of surprises and that nothing can protect us from adversity, although proper planning can lessen the devastation of its impact.

As her daughter grew, Karen continued to manage the finances, spending thoughtfully, saving aggressively and investing wisely. Even throughout the ups and downs of marriage and family she remained focused on their financial goals. By identifying their priorities of work and diversion she and Juan maintained a lifestyle they both enjoyed. They traveled extensively as a hobby, bought a nice house, although not a mansion, and chose to drive nice cars, but not expensive imports.

Their daughter, Amy, grew up to be a competitive equestrian with Olympic dreams that they were able to financially support. Tall and lanky, she looked elegant astride the two talented horses they owned. Amy and Karen traveled the country for competitions that brought Amy closer to her dream. She was a great student and was able to get a terrific education. Due to her many absences for her competitions Karen and Juan kept her in private schools that worked with her around her travel schedule.

Juan and Karen were also committed to creating a substantial college fund for Amy so that she could continue with college, and if desired, graduate school. They were even able to set aside some money for each of their five nieces and nephews. And, eventually they reached their goal of having five million dollars in assets.

Amy chose to attend a private college near home so that she could continue with her equestrian training. During her freshman year, she suffered her first setback. Her Olympic hopeful horse that had been her daily companion for six years died from a veterinary error. The whole family was devastated. While grieving, Amy continued with school and tried to focus her energy on her younger horse.

But only three months later, their lives were turned completely inside out. At the age of eighteen, Amy had a massive stroke that paralyzed the entire left side of her body. Fortunately, she could still speak and displayed little neurological affects; but what was thought to be a well-planned future was now a black void.

While trying to deal with the emotional shock of her stroke, they also had to consider the financial aspects of this catastrophic health situation. Many times throughout their lives they had considered lowering insurance costs by paring down health insurance. Why not? They were all healthy and took good care of themselves through daily exercise and healthy eating habits. But Karen's work in the political arena of health care helped her realize that the true test of a health policy is the benefits you would receive if something truly awful happened. And with the assistance of her team of professionals, she helped Juan understand that good health coverage, just like life and disability insurance, is an investment to insure financial security during possible illness. With Amy facing eight to ten weeks in the hospital, a week of which was in intensive care, and in-house rehabilitation, they knew the bills would be hefty.

During the first few days of Amy's recovery in the neurological intensive care unit, they were also told that a contributing factor to Amy's stroke was an undetected congenital heart defect that would require heart surgery. They were fortunate that their insurance would cover almost all of these massive health care bills so that they could focus on what they needed to do to help their daughter in her long, uncertain recovery.

The family focus changed from supporting their daughter in her Olympic dream to supporting her in her physical and emotional rehabilitation process. Amy endured long hours of physical rehabilitation, eventually graduating from being bedridden, to getting around in a wheel chair, walking with a cane, and then walking with a slight limp. All those years of intense training had taught Amy focus and tenacity. She needed those skills to endure neurological evaluation and training and to recover from a frightening major heart operation. She persevered despite her pain and the emotional anguish of physical disability and dependence. She was often exhausted by the regular activities of daily living. She had to learn to live using just one arm and hand. Tasks like drying and styling her hair, opening containers and cutting her food often overwhelmed her, but Amy's strength kept her and her family going.

Amy only missed one semester of college. She got right back into the summer session despite her physical challenges. At this point, she could walk short distances, but could not use her left arm or hand. But she kept on fighting. She attacked school with the same fierceness that she had attacked her Olympic dreams.

But the tragedy had other adverse results that Juan and Karen had never envisioned. Adversity affects everyone differently. Part of Juan's reaction to the crisis was deciding to end the marriage of twenty-five years. Karen was devastated, angry, and afraid. Her parents had been married for fifty-five years when her mother died, and she had hoped for the same in her life. She immediately enlisted the support of her financial team to evaluate her future. Somehow, despite the gaping wound in her heart and soul, she was able to focus on the business of divorce. She decided that she had to treat this matter as she would the breakup of a partnership. Juan was the CEO and she was the CFO.

The years of preparation, thoughtful spending and wise investing paid off. She had an intimate knowledge of their finances and had spent time and energy learning about investing. She knew that she had to plan carefully throughout the divorce process so that she wouldn't suffer a major financial blow. Many women end up with the short end of the finances in divorce, and she was not going to let that happen to her. Juan would leave the divorce with his tremendous earning power intact. Since she had tempered her work choices with the priority of the family's needs, she was unsure of her ability to reenter the job market.

Her determination to understand the finances throughout her marriage served her well in the divorce proceedings. She was able to identify which assets would best create her future financial picture. Once again, with her financial team, she knew more of what her needs were than either of her outstanding attorneys. Since she was financially savvy, she was able to negotiate a far superior settlement for herself. She realized that cash or cash-producing assets suited her future needs best. Once identified, she concentrated on obtaining them in the settlement.

After she received these assets, she had to focus on a totally different investment plan. She needed a comfortable guaranteed income and long-term financial security for her and her daughter. She also wanted to consider her future health needs. And, she wanted to incorporate asset protection given today's litigious culture.

Although her heart still aches at the loss of her dream of a nuclear family, she is proud to have accomplished her financial goals. In the months following her divorce, she built a new house without incurring any debt; maintained life insurance to provide for her daughter; and had a comfortable guaranteed income that let her pursue her traveling hobby and other dreams. Although she is still nursing emotional wounds, she is now preparing to tackle a new career.

She has learned first hand that adversity can be devastating. But knowing that her financial house is in order has relieved her of the fear of "becoming a little old lady surviving on cat food." That sense of financial confidence has given her the time and space to grieve and given her the ability to pursue her dreams.

Married to a Wealthy Business Owner

Anita, who is thirty-nine years old, "has been married forever it seems" to Jon. They grew up together in a Chicago suburb and were high school and college sweethearts. Anita describes them as a "comfortable team" because they grew up together and knew each other like a book. They shared similar drives and ambitions. Anita was an astute vice president with a public relations firm before she had their daughter. Jon was a graduate of a prominent business school and was on a fast track after completing his MBA.

Anita recalled, "Time had flown by; we were both engrossed in our careers, and Jon was concentrating on the business. I woke up one day realizing I wasn't getting any younger, and if there was a time to start a family, it was today. Nine months later Miriam was born. I was in my mid-thirties then." Now Anita's life centers around "enjoying Miriam and doing things Moms do."

Jon has become very successful in their garment business, and they live in one of the prestigious villages outside Chicago. Anita also is involved with "obligatory society bashes at the club" although she would rather be home reading. Her humble beginnings make her conservative; she considers herself to be "a brunette with a brain" rather than "a showy bauble at the end of a husband's arm." Jon "gives her a hefty allowance each month," but Anita would rather spend money on antiques, the gardener, and other items "to create house beautiful" than spend money on expensive clothes and personal items. Jon buys her diamonds for each major occasion, and her collection is "to die for." Their daughter is growing, and Anita cannot believe how many years she has been out of the business world!

Anita describes Jon as "a good provider. He is the most intense and driven man I know." She says, "his 'old world drive' is evidenced in everything he does. How he manipulates vendors, engineers processes to work, has his shoes shined, placates non-influential people, and controls influential ones. For Jon, the words "no" or "can't" do not exist. He is obsessed with money and power to the point that he truly believes that he can buy anything he needs or wants, anytime he wants it. He must have the best and biggest of everything—houses, cigars, wine, clothes, cars, and women."

Anita recalls incredulously, "It's the women that I never bargained for. And the wife is always the last to know. I knew about his secretary for a long time. But that was discreet and behind closed doors. But after he became successful and power-ful, he didn't care what people thought anymore. He lost all dis-cretion. Jon never thought I knew. His jilted secretary told me everything after she was replaced with another woman. 'Hell hath no fury like a woman scorned.'"

Anita had more courage and foresight regarding "the rich man/other woman syndrome" than any woman whom I have ever worked with. She resolved, "Power corrupts and absolute power cor-rupts absolutely. I'm just biding my time. The hardest thing I have to deal with is posing as the dutiful wife with the humiliation of every-one thinking that I don't know what Jon is doing, or thinking that I'm sitting back and accepting it. My time will come. But for now Miriam needs a father, and I have plenty of time . . . But from this point for-ward, *I* am going to become very visible—in everything."

Anita respected her husband's business ability; he has devoted his life to it. She knows, however, that the details of suc-cession planning have not been completed. His energy had been spent on making the business grow and not in the area of protect-ing the business or his family in case of his death or disability. He also drinks and smokes and truly believes his success and power in business in some way make him physically indestructible.

Anita began to review the financial details of her family and the business. The business has an outstanding loan of $750,000; it is secured by a life insurance policy assigned to the bank. Therefore, if Jon dies, the insurance will pay the loan.

Jon has no disability income protection because he truly believes the business could support him if he became disabled. What he does not realize is that if he is not actively working, the paycheck he receives from the business may be considered as a company dividend for income tax purposes. Therefore, the business may not deduct his paycheck, unless he has a formal wage continuation arrangement in place to explain how much he would receive and how long he would receive it. Neither his accountant nor financial professional has explained this.

Jon has a $1 million term life insurance policy of which Anita is beneficiary. Anita also learned that Jon also has two $500,000 cash value life insurance policies with other women named as beneficiaries.

There is no formal pension or other retirement plan at Jon's business. His old world ideas have instilled a mindset that truly believes that *the value of the business will be the retirement benefit*; it would be sold, and he would live off the proceeds. To this date, profits have been put back into the business for updating equipment, marketing efforts, and increasing staff to keep up with growth.

When Anita began to discuss finances and the business with Jon, he admitted that he wasn't personally involved in estate and pension planning; he made it known that he does not have the physical time to coordinate a financial program—"that's what he pays his attorney for." He also believed that he had enough life insurance; he's never sick; therefore, he doesn't need disability income protection, and he doesn't think he'll ever retire because he's "making too much money—why retire?"

When Anita told Jon she was going to get involved with the business finances, he wasn't overly receptive, but did not deny her doing it either. She asked him to introduce her to the attorney, CPA, and financial professional because there were "a few things [she] wanted to understand better." Jon also admitted to not being exact about the business value but estimated it at approximately $3 million.

Needs

If, like Anita, you are married to a wealthy business owner and desire to become more familiar than you have been about how you and your children are protected in addition to how the business is protected, you will want to become knowledgeable about the following:

♦ Ask to be introduced to the attorney, CPA, and financial professional and meet with them as a team. Ask them to come prepared to the meeting with copies of all wills, trust documents, corporate and personal tax returns, and summaries for all insurance policies and investment statements.

♦ You want to understand the status of the business and your personal finances as a family. The purpose of this meeting is for you to tell them, "treat this visit as though I had just been widowed." You are asking them for their professional recommendations about any measures they should be taking to protect the business and personal or business assets.

♦ Ask the attorney how the business is structured and if your husband died what effect it would have on you, your family and the business.

♦ Learn from the attorney if there have been any trusts or wills written.

♦ Ask the attorney if there has been any estate tax planning done.

♦ Ask the attorney what type of exposure the business has to lawsuit.

♦ Ask the CPA if there has been a business valuation done and to explain the last five-year's corporate and personal tax returns.

♦ Ask the financial professional to provide a complete update regarding all insurance in place as well as to explain the benefits your husband presently has through the corporation.

♦ Ask the financial professional to review all the insurance policies in place and who is beneficiary. You need to know how much there is for you as beneficiary. Oftentimes, a wife is told by her husband, "I have $3 million of life insurance." But he may not explain who is the owner and who is the beneficiary. The wife believes that she has $3 million plus the business. This is often not the case because the insurance is assigned to the business.

♦ Ask the financial professional to explain what retirement planning has been done and how the investments have performed.

Often business owners have a grand idea that the value of the business *is* their retirement and that they will sell the business for $1 million to have security in their retirement years. Anita worried about this because she saw her uncle lose everything he had invested when the vinyl record industry collapsed to make way for new technology several years ago. She needs to anticipate what would happen if the business suffers great loss and the business loses its book values because its market or technology become obsolete overnight.

As a wife of a business owner, you should approach your understanding of the business as if you were widowed and left with the business and the responsibility of home and children. You need to know if there are employees who are trained and knowledgeable to run the business or if you will need to hire executive talent to help you to keep the business together. This is probably not realistic considering the fact that your husband's business was successful because of the successful relationships he built over the years. The business would suffer extreme losses while you try to begin new or to maintain those existing relationships on your own. In the meantime, there most likely would be a domestic or offshore competitor already knocking at the door of your customers while you are in mourning.

Married to a Principal in a Professional Firm

When death occurs in businesses such as professional corporations involving doctors, lawyers, or accountants, no one can step in and take over the role of the deceased partner other than a someone who is licensed in the business. As a wife and widow, you could be responsible for patient or client files, office expenses, and employees, and you could have no other choice but to sell the business. This process takes months, during which the business expenses must be paid. If you hope to sell the business and client base at a profit, the business must be a worthwhile investment to purchase, and, therefore, it must be operational and running while it is for sale.

The employees, patients, or clients must be assured on a daily basis that there will be a new doctor, lawyer, or CPA to provide the same care and skill as your husband once gave them. If not, they will all go elsewhere, leaving you as a widow without any business to sell.

Questions to Ask

Anita's desire to become involved in understanding the financials of the business can begin by working with the attorney, CPA, and financial professional who make up her husband's professional team. Anita's perseverance to obtain the necessary knowledge should prove to be an incredible asset. Here are specific questions to explore:

- ♦ In how many years does your husband wish to retire?
- ♦ Is there a succession arrangement in order at the business that provides for new management when he retires?
- ♦ Is there short- and long-term debt on the business?
- ♦ Has there been a business valuation done? What are the annual receivables?
- ♦ What income does your husband receive from the business?
- ♦ Is there a pension plan in order at the business?
- ♦ How much life insurance is there on your husband's life? How many separate policies exist?
- ♦ Who is listed as beneficiary of his life insurance?
- ♦ As a business owner, does your husband have an income protection policy?
- ♦ Does your husband have a disability overhead expense protection program that can help cover the cost of monthly business expenses in the event that he becomes disabled and qualifies for benefits? This is not available to all businesses.
- ♦ What type of wills and trusts are in order with your attorney?
- ♦ Are you knowledgeable about any estate planning that has been prepared for your family?
- ♦ Do you have your own life insurance?
- ♦ How long have you been married? Do you have a happy marriage? What would happen to you if he divorced you in order to marry his secretary?

Anita's Strategy

When Anita came to my office and shared her story and concerns, I suggested that she embark on this process as if she were a widow who is faced with these issues for real. Jon had given her full authority, and she was eager to begin. She stated, "It will be a tremendous learning curve, so I'll do it now while I am strong and before I'm faced with either death or divorce."

If Anita is widowed today, the total value of the estate needs to be known. Anita's attorney did a thorough study of potential estate tax issues and suggested an insurance trust for estate tax planning purposes. The attorney and the CPA gave suggested ideas about succession planning for the business in the event that Jon dies. The manufacturing plant has an approximate $3 million valuation as long as he is there operating it. A great deal of the value is in equipment and inventory. But if these assets are sold to liquidate the business in the event of Jon's death, they may only earn 50 cents on the dollar. Therefore, in the event Jon dies, the value of the business is more likely $1.5 million. It is recommended that Jon consider finding a talented, young, spirited successor to carry on the business operations to keep a steady flow of contracts and jobs producing revenue.

I recommended that a new life insurance policy be placed inside the insurance trust. The value of the business as well as home and other assets would create an estate tax issue. Life insurance inside the trust can help Anita have an income and help pay estate taxes.

Anita needs to remember that women generally outlive men. While planning, she needs to think as though she is a widow who will live with the plans that Jon put in place. Now is the opportunity to obtain the peace of mind and to verify that all issues have been addressed and satisfied.

By building relationships with the professional team, Anita can stay involved and keep a keen eye on the growth of the business and its impact on her and Miriam's futures. She can also continue to keep a keen eye on Jon.

Wealthy in Your Own Right

Jane

When thinking about the wealthy women I have worked with over the years, I have great pride in those who have truly created and accumulated their own wealth. There are many successful entrepreneurs throughout the country whom I am concerned about as well. Have they spent the same amount of time being personally accountable for their financial affairs as they have spent time building their image and their empire? Do they have a trusting and loyal professional team? Do they have regular meetings with their attorneys, financial professionals, and CPAs to review their personal finances as they have regular meetings to review their bookings and schedules? How many successful American women are earning wealth and losing it? How many models, actresses, TV personalities, singers, musicians, and athletes are turning over their financial futures to others because they themselves have no time to become knowledgeable and personally accountable for their financial affairs? Are they controlling their own assets, or have they delegated them "to their booking agent to handle?" Is someone else writing checks on her account and making decisions that will ultimately affect the wealthy woman's future long after retirement when she no longer has the benefit of her beauty, her body, her company, her product, or her pretty face?

My client, Jane, is a successful actress who made her debut on *Dallas*. We met years after her career was solidly established. She had concerns about her money, but did not know where or how to begin. The only person she had trusted in life had passed away; her father was her idol, her friend, and her confidant. Jane felt guilty about her success. She discussed what she called "the fatal irony of her life." She confided, "I know that actresses are in the public and media eye. For it is the public, paparazzi, and the critics who make us or break us. Often our sense of self-worth or whole identity is determined by whether our movie was well received by the public, the critics, or the media. We hate being owned by the public, and we desperately seek a very private life."

Her father knew the entertainment industry and taught her that there are ways to avoid *probate* (which is the process during which creditors are paid off and assets are distributed after a person's death.) The administrative fees of probate can be costly. Probate exposes the entire process to the world since all proceedings are a matter of public record and available to anyone at the local county courthouse. Jane recited the story as if her father had made her memorize it by rote. Marilyn Monroe's untimely death left an estate in probate for almost eighteen years. After her death, royalties on her image and movies soared and earned her estate more than $1.6 million dollars. During that time, there were substantial expenses, and her beneficiaries only received a small portion of the original estate.

We discussed Jane's concerns to the point where she felt comfortable with the understanding that putting insurance inside a trust keeps its value from adding to the value of her estate. Insurance also can be used to help pay the taxes on her estate so her heirs would not experience a significant loss in the worth of the estate after the estate tax is paid nine months after her death.

Jane also recited the Bing Crosby story her father told her. When Bing Crosby's first wife, Dixie, passed away in the 1950s, Bing had to sell some of their assets to pay the taxes. At that time, there was no unlimited marital deduction. Because of the community property laws, the probate records indicated the exact descriptions and amounts of all of Crosby's holdings. Bing was very upset by how the press seized the information and told the world. He later established a *living trust* that kept the value of his estate and holdings private when he died. In fact, to this day, no one but the family really knows how his assets were distributed or how large his estate was at the time of his death. Bing Crosby's estate planning goal was privacy, and a living trust enabled him to achieve that goal.

Jane's acting success, as well as the royalties and fees she earned on her movies and videos, had created a sizable revenue stream. Up to the time we met, Jane had designated the care of her income and investing to her talent agent. Her idea was that, "He assures me of the next job, so he has a vested interest to see that I make money."

Jane was comfortable with his guidance for the present. But she was uncomfortable with the idea for her long-term future. She was concerned about her later years when she was "eighty years old and no longer working," after her beauty was gone and her image was "no longer a commodity that a newer, younger generation adored."

Needs

If, like Jane, you are blessed with talent, beauty, success, and the wealth these bring, do not be so busy with the trappings of everyday life that you delegate decisions about your personal financial future. *As a wealthy woman in your own right you must be personally involved because you more than anyone have the most to lose.* You need:

♦ To become knowledgeable of the financial world.
♦ To personally select your own professional team of a CPA, attorney, and financial professional whom you know you can trust and who are willing to teach you as you grow and develop a long-term relationship.
♦ To begin to learn about investment vehicles, stocks, bonds, mutual funds, variable annuities, and the like.
♦ To determine goals and a greater purpose for your wealth.
♦ To understand how wealth can create significant tax issues.
♦ To become knowledgeable about estate tax planning, charitable remainder trusts, insurance trusts, family trusts, asset protection, and many others.
♦ To preserve the empire you have created.
♦ To be personally involved rather than delegate the responsibility of your future at an old age to any one other person. Do not let anyone sign checks without your approval.

Questions to Ask

♦ Are you confident that the members of your professional team are available and willing to teach you?
♦ If you are single, where do you want your money to go when you die? Determine if you want to give cash to many nonproductive

relatives or would you prefer to set up a foundation or give to an existing charitable institution?

♦ If you are married or have children, have you done what is necessary to help preserve the empire for your spouse and/or children and minimize payment of estate taxes?

♦ What is your estate valued at today?

♦ What are your investment accounts worth? Who will receive the accounts when you die? Insist that your financial professional give you quarterly or updated reports.

♦ What is the value of each of your real estate holdings?

♦ Is there a master record of all holdings including: address; name assigned to title, lease, or contract; present value; and, copy of the deed or title?

♦ How much life insurance do you have, and who are beneficiaries?

♦ What type of trusts are in order?

♦ If you died today, would your family or friends know what to do and who to call?

♦ Are all of your financial assets recorded with name of title, location, and account number?

♦ How long does your current contract guarantee your income?

♦ Is your income stream or wealth related to political or other power factors that can be easily jeopardized?

♦ Is your wealth related to athletic or physical performance that can be limited by a certain length of time when you are considered to be in the prime of your career?

♦ How much of your cash flow derives from investments in other business operations?

Jane's Strategy

Jane needed to begin at the beginning and was nervous about it. We detailed a list of action items that she needed to pursue once she was comfortable with assuming the responsibility.

She first needed to select a professional team with whom she would feel comfortable. She knew that in the future she wanted to have hands-on involvement regarding all financial decisions that will ultimately affect her estate and retirement.

Her CPA would help in the valuation of her assets, real estate holdings, investments, rights, and royalties as well as be responsible for organizing a report summary.

She decided to select a new attorney, rather than retain her father's family attorney. She wanted someone experienced in the entertainment industry and in estate planning. The attorney would get her estate in order by drafting the proper trust so that estate taxes could be minimized.

Checks and Balances among Professional Team

As her financial professional, I assisted in estate planning and asset protection. I suggested that we meet with the attorney to discuss a *charitable remainder trust* that offers creative tax advantages. Jane's estate was worth $18 million. Jane considered a series of concepts applicable to sizable estates: charitable remainder trusts, revocable and irrevocable life insurance trusts, asset protection for liability reasons, and family limited partnerships. Together, the attorney and I worked with Jane to diagnose her needs according to tax planning and wealth preservation priorities.

Jane has committed to meet with me, her CPA, and attorney on a regular basis. We are her principal team who coordinate the rest of her financial professionals. We provide her with records of all of her holdings, teach her how her holdings and investments are diversified, coordinate and implement a properly designed insurance program, and provide updates on present investment values.

Checks and balances occurs among the professional team as we each discuss our perspectives on problems and possible solutions regarding Jane's estate. We meet each quarter prior to our group meeting with Jane. This enables us to prepare and present a cohesive approach to Jane regarding current and future issues impacting her wealth. Our opinions offer a wide range of expertise to create coordinated strategies and ways to implement her future plans. We also helped Jane to identify additional key players who are most likely to be involved during Jane's life and career. The attorney who specializes in contract rights, royalties, and the entertainment industry; the chief financial officer of her corporation; her tax planning attorney; and her investment portfolio manager are called upon as needed.

The woman with true wealth has a complexly detailed task in managing a course for her wealth. To simplify the course can mean the difference between her having or losing wealth. She needs to be at the helm, in control of the crew, steering the course—not the maiden figurehead or beautiful face along for the ride. For in a storm, she is first and hardest hit when the ship wrecks.

10
To Retire

Working Woman Retiring

"I worked hard all my life; with no one to help me, and I'm looking forward to not working, so I can have time when I can make myself the main priority every day." That was Rea's admission when she came to my office for retirement planning at age sixty-five. Rea was referred to me by her fifty-year-old sister; I helped her understand her husband's pension and annuity benefit payout options.

Rea worked all her life as an executive secretary and administrative assistant for a large corporation. She is a tall and slender horsewoman who loved Texas, horses, and kids, in that order. Her reputation of teaching and mentoring kids to make them work well with animals was known far and wide. She had worked and championed 4-H programs in Fort Worth and lived near her sister and brother-in-law. Rea's eyes danced when she talked about the riding students she had over the years—George was her favorite. "That good lookin' kid with that smile you'd remember forever; he learned that famous Texas two-step in a rodeo, and he's still singin' with it in his heart."

She was excited about retirement. However, she did not understand the pension materials her company provided. She was frightened because she never had financial guidance over the years. She did not feel she had the knowledge and expertise to make an informed decision regarding money matters that would affect the rest of her life.

Rea confided that she had no children or husband. Her lifestyle was modest and uncomplicated. Her social life consisted of equestrian and church activities and walking outdoors. She absolutely loved the subtle beauty of the high desert ranch lands of Texas and spent a great deal of time telling me about how she would paint watercolors of her favorite scenes so she could keep the image with her all year around—"fields of Texas bluebonnets; flocks of finches so plentiful, fine, and fair they'd turn a Cottonwood yellow."

"I've lived a simple life without too many sophisticated needs. But I want the perspective of someone who deals with these matters every day. Someone who can explain all the options to me," insisted Rea. She wanted to be taught; she wanted materials to read; she wanted explanations; she wanted to know all the reasons why something was recommended, and she wanted time to distill the information before making any decisions.

Needs

If, like Rea, you are approaching retirement, you'll want to consider the following:

- ◆ To become debt free.
- ◆ To have a mortgage paid.
- ◆ To have a better understanding of your fixed expenses.
- ◆ To have a better understanding of Social Security benefits.
- ◆ To have a full understanding of your pension and payout options.

Questions to Ask

- ◆ Do you have an understanding of your Social Security and what your monthly benefits will be?
- ◆ Do you understand pension values and the amount you will receive?
- ◆ Can you take your pension in a lump sum?
- ◆ Do you understand all of your pension options?
- ◆ What are your fixed expenses?
- ◆ What are your plans and goals for your retirement years (e.g. write a book, travel, buy a vacation home)?

Rea's Strategy

Rea first needed a financial professional who was willing to review her company pension materials and explain them thoroughly.

The best years of Rea's career were the last two when she earned an annual salary of $45,000. Earlier, she had bought a Chevy Silverado pickup truck knowing it would last her until she died. She paid it off and last year bought and paid for her Appaloosa and a horse trailer. Rea had been saving for ten years and was proud to have her dream come true at last and to have it paid for in cash. Rea had paid the mortgage on her 1,500 square foot Texas ranch house when she was in her forties, so she was happy to be retiring without debt. Her monthly expenses were $1,500.

Upon review, her pension statement showed an annuity payout of $1,500 monthly and an $18,000 annual income for as long as Rea lives. If Rea had a spouse she could exercise an option to take less per month and guarantee an income to her spouse after she died. Since Rea is single, she will take the maximum allowed with the reassurance of having this monthly income for as long as she lives.

Let's look at her married sister's situation. Her husband wished to elect an annuity *payout option* upon retirement in fifteen years. For a married couple, a $3,000 monthly pension payment option can be handled in a number of ways.

- The employee monthly receives 100 percent of the annuity calculation, $3,000, for a lifetime. The benefit is the maximum monthly income. The drawback is that when her husband dies, the spouse has no income. Therefore, if a couple elects to receive the payout at 100 percent, they often purchase a life insurance policy that can provide the monthly income upon death of the employee (in this case the husband), that would have equaled the same amount as if the husband had elected the spousal payout option. (This concept is often referred to as *pension maximization*.)
- Another way is for the employee to take the *spousal annuity option*. This allows the couple to have less income than the 100 percent annuity calculation. Then, when the employee dies, the spouse will receive a calculated portion of the full amount.

Because Rea was alone, single, and without children who might look after her in her old age, she was concerned about her final years and elected to purchase a *long-term care* policy. She chose one with both nursing home and in-home health care benefits.

Rea chose to save her Social Security check of $600 per month and invest it in mutual funds. Her goal was to accumulate $10,000 in a money market account for emergency needs. After that, the monthly contributions were placed in growth and income funds.

We also made arrangements to transfer the $160,000 available in her 401(k) pension fund into a variable annuity that offers growth potential. Rea can access these funds any time when necessary later in life. In the event Rea became incapacitated, the annuity can help provide for her care. A custodian or other individual may have to be designated in order for them to access the policy. Upon Rea's death, any balance will be bequeathed to the 4-H Club.

Rea was overjoyed to have her affairs "in order" as she called it. She was free to make time for what she loved—free to ride among flocks of finches in fields of Texas bluebonnets so fine and fair.

11
To Pass Wealth on to Heirs

Widow

— *Betty* —

Betty never thought she would be a widow at age sixty-nine—for a second time. Her young groom was killed in the Korean War, and she waited many years to remarry. At age fifty, she married a younger man. She believed, "I wanted to marry someone younger whom I thought would outlive me because I never wanted to go through the pain of loss again. I never thought I would be widowed again."

At this point in her life, she did not have the emotional strength to remarry, even though she was "still young." She felt deeply about not ever being a burden to her daughter. She was very independent and lived on a fixed income.

She is doing fine financially because her husband had set up a trust from which she receives a monthly income. She likes the fact that she does not have to worry because he did a very good job of planning. She has three grandchildren, and she desires to live modestly, so that someday she will be able to pass on an inheritance to her daughter and grandchildren.

Needs

The months following the death of a faithful companion are heart wrenching, but eventually all the world becomes new again. If, like Betty, you are a widow, you will want to ask questions and consider these important next steps:

- ♦ To identify how assets are to be distributed after your death.
- ♦ To determine if estate taxes will be due.
- ♦ To have an updated will.
- ♦ To consider adding children to joint accounts.
- ♦ To obtain copies of trust and trust financial statements, life insurance company, address, financial professional/s, and phone number/s.
- ♦ To list names of attorney, CPA, and financial professional.
- ♦ To locate the deed or title to your home.
- ♦ To enumerate your desires on a wish list. Designate jewelry, personal items, furnishings that are special as gifts to specific loved ones.
- ♦ To have a heart-to-heart discussion with your children, explain your desires and review what is in place, the location of important papers with summary pages explaining Social Security numbers, bank, bank location, account numbers, safety deposit box and numbers.

Questions to Ask

- ♦ Do you have a long-term care program?
- ♦ Do you have a safety deposit box?
- ♦ Do you have any life insurance on yourself? If so, how much?
- ♦ Would you like to leave a legacy to your children or grandchildren?
- ♦ What investments do you have?
- ♦ Is your monthly income adequate?
- ♦ Do you have statutory or health care powers of attorney established?
- ♦ Have you updated your will since your husband's death? Do you have a living will drafted?
- ♦ Have you considered putting your children's names on any of your accounts?

Betty's Strategy

Betty has been taking interest from the trust fund her husband established. She has no debt and lives on $1,000 per month. Her husband made arrangements to provide her a lifetime income and pass the rest to her daughter upon Betty's death. Betty truly wants to leave the $175,000 trust fund to her daughter and grandchildren.

A portion of Betty's Social Security check has purchased a long-term care policy and has paid for the extras, gifts, and church contributions. Betty also had a cash value life insurance policy for $75,000 for which she has named her daughter beneficiary.

In addition, Betty has asked her daughter to purchase a $100,000 cash value life insurance policy on her mother. It is Betty's wish to leave $50,000 each to both grandchildren, and she is giving her daughter the money to pay the premiums. Life insurance at this stage in her life is a good way to provide her grandchildren this substantial sum of money on an income tax-free basis for less than $100,000.

In her heart, Betty knows that even though her mementos hold great importance to her, these will never have the same value to her heirs as $100,000 cash. The money will help the children in their financial direction in a way that mementos never will be able to help them. Her husband set affairs right for Betty, and it was her desire to do the same for her daughter and grandchildren.

Preserving Wealth for Children

Crucial legacy issues arise when a family grows an empire and passes it from generation to generation. Some families have accumulated wealth by methodical cash savings; other families have acquired, nurtured, and developed various forms of standing wealth. Many families own standing wealth such as real estate, farms, or ranch lands.

Sharon and Rob were introduced to me by a friend who was aware of their concerns about their land holdings. Sharon and Rob grew up together on adjacent ranches and eventually married. Their union and inheritance created one of the largest spreads on the Great Plains.

Their 33,000-acre ranch has a meandering river where Sharon often sits on the bank to fish and to collect her thoughts. When we met there, Sharon had tears in her eyes as she told me about how she recently helped her best friend, Linda, the day that Linda's family was forced to auction off their ranch to pay estate taxes after her mother died. Linda's ranch had been in the family since 1805, and "nine generations of little ones had slept in grandma's feather bed." But the day had come when they lost it all. All of their possessions were on the front lawn, including tractors, machinery, a herd of Texas Longhorns, a herd of two hundred wild mustangs that had sanctuary on the ranch, as well as work horses used for roundups. There were twenty-four ranch hands who watched their world come to an end. It all was auctioned—livestock, possessions, parcels of land, house—and grandma's feather bed. A legacy spanning almost two hundred years was gone in twelve hours.

Sharon never wanted that to happen to her children. She was deeply concerned about one child who was suffering from drug addiction. The others were young and irresponsible and were taking the wealth of their land for granted.

Sharon and Rob live off the ranch and the land. They raise cattle for the stockyards; their garden and orchards provide all necessary foodstuffs. They work the land for survival—for themselves and four children. Sharon's wealth is the value of the land rather than any income it generates.

Sharon heard from a neighboring rancher about how his family had been working with an attorney to use *gifting* to give the land to the children in order to help reduce the estate value for tax purposes. This option didn't appeal to her because her children were not behaving responsibly. She had also heard about *family limited partnerships*. Therefore, she wanted to discuss these with her attorney as well as other estate planning concepts that would allow her and Rob to control the future of the estate during their lifetime and for generations to come long after she and Rob died.

Needs

If like Sharon, your livelihood is tied to standing wealth that is not generating income and is not easily liquidated, you need:

♦ To be involved in knowing the financials of the estate, particularly the profit and loss of goods and services at market to determine if ranching, farming, or other ventures are profitable.

♦ To have frequent communication with the real estate broker, attorney and CPA regarding the value of the land or property.

♦ To select and use a local CPA who is familiar with your type of property, holdings, and operations (such as ranch land, urban real estate, orchards, or vineyards), rather than rely on someone who may not be familiar with the local values of your ventures in other geographic locations.

♦ To work with the CPA to understand the impact of estate taxes for children when parents die.

♦ To work with your attorney to create a family limited partnership and to explore additional gifting options.

♦ To work with your financial professional to ensure that adequate liability coverage exists and that proper life insurance is in place for estate planning purposes and legacy wishes.

Questions to Ask

♦ What is the total income projection from all sources?

♦ What is the present value of the land holdings?

♦ What, if any, estate planning has been done?

♦ Is there insurance in an insurance trust to cover estate taxes?

♦ Are you in the know and do you have a working relationship with the banker, attorney and financial professional?

♦ Have any liens been placed on the property over the years as collateral for loans on buildings, barns, equipment, livestock, seedlings? Have the liens been paid? Are more liens anticipated?

♦ What other personal debt are you holding?

♦ Is your marriage solid or do you fear a divorce?

♦ Have you created a will or discussed what you care to leave your children?

♦ Have you discussed family limited partnership arrangements with your attorney?

Sharon's and Rob's Strategy

Sharon and Rob have been coping with drug and alcohol depend-ency in their family. It is taking its toll on the family, and they have been focused on the turmoil of these present years and not had much time to think about the long-term future.

Sharon learned that their total holdings including land, ranch house, outbuildings and herds were valued at more than $13 mil-lion, and the children could be faced with paying estate taxes after the death of the second parent. After the outstanding liens were sat-isfied, there would be no money to pay the taxes; the children would have to parcel out the ranch and sell it. (If a property involves lease-holds, the issues are even more complex regarding federal estate tax. It is imperative that a business valuation consultant be working with the attorney and tax specialist, in this case.)

Family Limited Partnership

The attorney proceeded to do estate tax planning and recommended that Sharon and Rob set up a family limited partnership. The first advantage of the family limited partnership is that the parents can give away wealth without giving up control over the assets. A second advantage is that the transfer (i.e., gift) of the limited partnership interests to younger generations can often be valued at a discount, which should be determined by your tax advisor. Finally, if stated in the partnership agreement, the limited partners cannot transfer their limited partnership interests except with the consent of the general partner and then only to other family members.

I further recommended a *second-to die life insurance* policy for which the family limited partnership is owner and beneficiary. It would provide the benefit to the children, as limited partners, upon the death of the second parent. The father and the mother are insured together by the same life insurance contract. The under-writing process considers risk spread over the life expectancy of both individuals. Rob had been experiencing blood pressure prob-lems, but Sharon's good health enabled them to receive a non-rated policy. Sharon and Rob purchased a $6 million sec-ond-to-die policy and will continue to monitor the value of the estate and the amount of insurance necessary to satisfy the estate taxes after the second insured dies.

Sharon and Rob, fearing "deep pockets syndrome," also increased their liability coverage because they feared exposure to lawsuit in the event that their teenagers, involved with drugs and alcohol, experienced driving accidents in which friends were injured or killed.

All of their planning with their professional team was to help realize the hope that no developers will ever divide the land, hunt the game, fish the rivers, or drill the oil on the ranch land they've had in their families for generations.

American lore is colored by tales of the great families of the Western Plains who have struggled to keep vast farmlands in the family for generations. There are families who have carved wealth from land rich with mineral rights or timberlands. Other great families have built and developed monumental estates and game preserves. Others have real estate, trading, banking, or industrial empires.

In America, the pioneer spirit and ability to homestead and live off the land evoke emotions and passions of epic proportions. Rich are the stories of families from the grasslands of the Great Plains; cattle ranches thick with mesquite and high chaparral westward from Texas to California; great timberlands of the Atlantic and Pacific north country; great tobacco and cotton plantations of the American South; fertile orchards and vineyards of the Pacific Coast; and the ranches, pineapple groves, and sugar plantations on our island states and territories. Such standing American wealth was built on sweat, love, and passion. It was built by blood and tears, war and conquest.

The spirit of wealth grows even stronger when families with large land holdings struggle to stem short-term economic trials in order to preserve the empire for their children and dream that their children marry to merge wealth. From *The Big Valley* to the

Ponderosa, Americans have been excited about this fiction in books and movies for generations.

Didi Devon is sassy, spirited, and attractive with a mind of her own. She knows what she wants, and nothing will stop her from getting it. Her father is a rancher who owns half the valley over the Spring Mountains in western Nevada. She wants to paint and see the world. The dusty, arid ranch with its relentless heat and harsh winds is nice to visit, but no place to realize her dreams; she doesn't want to spend the rest of her life in a place with nothing but cattle, lizards, and jack rabbits.

Down the valley there's the Darling ranch. Dick Darling is lanky, blond, handsome, and ambitious. His hard-working hands have talents to bring him the world and any woman he wants. He's leery of women gold diggers out for his land and his oil. He left his ranch to travel the world and seek fortune on his own. His grandfather owns the cattle ranch and oil rights. The parents want these two to marry and merge their joining lands; hopefully, it would settle these spirited youngsters down, keep them both closer to Nevada—for the good of the family. Their union would keep outside interests from buying the land in future years.

Together Didi and Dick could live happily ever after. They could own the whole valley; they could name their ranch the "Big Double D."

But after time with Dick, Didi realizes he's fun to be with, but she could never love him—a man who is always late and always has dirty hands, a man whose trucks, equipment, and business deals will always be more important than giving her the things she wants. Didi's mind and ambition are somewhere else. She wants a man with money, not a man who needs to work for it.

In his heart, Dick knows but won't admit that Didi can never give him the friendship, loyalty, love, and passion that he once had with Jane. Jane still adores him and is giving him all the time he needs to realize she is the only woman who truly loves him for what he is—not for what he can give her. His heart still remembers her dancing eyes and dark beauty in a phosphorescent tide on Horseshoe Bay along the pink sand in Bermuda, at another time. He quietly regrets buckling under family pressure to leave her. Jane was self-made with money of her own, not after his. She loved him honestly, completely. She made him smile and made him happy. They were great for each other. With her, he could conquer the world, and together they could accomplish even more with a flame that consumes the darkness.

Dick and Didi come close to marriage, but she admits he's not enough; she wants more, and Dick still can't get Jane out of his mind. The heart wants what the heart wants. Dick finally realizes that behind a successful man is a passionate woman and that Jane truly is the only woman who could ever love him exactly the way he is. No other woman can replace what he had with Jane. But would she wait? Would she still be there for him after all these years?

You know the story. You've seen the movie. The parents are heart-broken and left angry to die among the tumbleweed. Without influx of new capital and new blood, the ranch is sold. Paradise is paved and outside interests put up a parking lot.

It will take more than marriage between the next generation to preserve the Devon and Darling legacies.

For large estates and families who have accumulated wealth, financial planning is essential. It is how the American Dream lives on—from generation to generation.

EPILOGUE

— Barbara —

Barbara was fifty-two years old when she was referred to me by her attorney in 1993. In the early days of building her business, she had struggled as a single parent. Barbara was determined never to go backwards and began to tell me about how far she had really come to get to this point.

"I'll never forget the day in my small Oklahoma town when I walked in tears from the courtroom; I was thirty-seven years old and no longer a married woman. It was April 4, 1977, the day after my wedding anniversary. In one morning, I was suddenly a single parent with two teenage sons who needed a great deal of love, nurturing, and guidance. An overwhelming sensation engulfed me—I would be doing this alone as well as exerting all my energies to live as a single woman. Back in 1977, the ERA had not yet emerged as a household word!

"As I drove to my apartment, my thoughts were on savings, college education, and retirement; however, the impending bills and everyday cost of living took over my imagination and quickly caused me to focus on the present. Important decisions needed to be made that would have an impact on all of us. The most important goal at that point was to be able to move home to Texas within a year. My parents lived there, and I thought it valuable to have family support nearby.

"The days ambled along, and I continued to work in a job that was interesting, but had very little potential. My children were involved in school and community activities. Our lives were adjusting to the divorce as well as I could possibly expect. I labored diligently to meet my goal and I saved whatever money I could by budgeting and by attempting several part-time jobs beyond my full-time employment. I could find no extra money to deposit in savings to meet emergency situations much less for anything beyond those.

"When we relocated to Texas, a position was offered to me. It increased my salary and produced a sense of security; nevertheless, it meant working for someone with less than a congenial attitude. Again my thoughts turned to providing for future needs, but how quickly these notions were diminished. I was overwhelmed from handling a new job, from establishing my sons in new schools, and from finding a place to live that we could call our own.

"On most evenings, the phone would ring and salesmen would inquire about my needs for insurance, financial planning, or burial plots. I dismissed these needs and took care of what I believed to be more urgent. It was the late 1970s, and my main concentration was to be awarded credit in my own name! In those days, being single and a woman made this almost impossible. My vow to obtain as many credit cards as possible soon became an avocation. The importance for a woman, single or married, to develop her own identity in terms of financial credit became a priority.

"In 1979, within a year of moving to Texas, I seized an opportunity to purchase a small day care center. My parents agreed to aid in the financing that made another adventure possible. I happily put aside seeking credit card acceptance and thrust myself into what I considered to be a second job. The anticipation of the day when the day care center could become my sole support turned my thoughts to further establish goals. Unfortunately, my boss felt that my work with my day care center was a conflict of interest, and I was suddenly without primary employment. The new adventure of day care as an income supplement suddenly shifted to a battle for survival. It was another giant step for womankind!"

After starting a new business, Barbara felt that this is what she should have been doing for years. She had found her niche. Six months later, in 1980, she moved the day care center into larger quarters. Her next personal goal was to complete state certification requirements and obtain licensing. After she became licensed, the day care grew to 130 children by the end of 1981. Within two years, the center grew by 300 percent. Barbara was great at the day-to-day care of children and overseeing staff, but she lacked knowledge about how to run a business. She knew she needed to stay in touch with her financial professional because it was important to increase coverage as her business grew. However, in 1986, four years after starting the business, the day care industry was dropped by all the top insurance companies.

Barbara remembered, "I was advised of the cancellation of my general liability policy and was told that several large insurance companies no longer insured day care centers. I panicked. My business would be unprotected. I could not lose what I had so diligently worked to build. Where would I go? Whom would I turn to? I joined a child care organization and started asking questions. Fortunately, I found people who knew what I was going through and what I needed. I was referred to a company and was able to be insured, but what a price I paid—both emotionally and financially!"

That incident changed Barbara's focus; she began to realize that she had to work with professionals who understood the needs of a small business owner. Barbara continued, "I did not feel that my CPA was experienced in business issues nor did she keep me well informed. I stopped doing business with her, and I actively pursued a new CPA and eventually found a tax attorney and financial professional.

"In 1986, my new attorney recommended that I have a will in order because I had not had one created since moving to Texas. In 1990, the attorney also recommended incorporation; it would give me more leverage for banking purposes. Since a day care business has a high exposure to liability, being incorporated also protected me against personal liability in the event that the business was sued.

"As I continued the long trek of becoming a successful entrepreneur, the importance of having a financial program to face emergencies and to save money became immediate. I purchased whole life insurance policies for me and my sons. These policies were not large, but they gave me a feeling of security that I was protecting the future for my children. After the death of my parents, I received an inheritance and launched my first step into mutual funds. This money also enabled me to bestow money to each son to aid in his future plans. With the mutual funds in place and a certificate of deposit I gained years ago from my divorce settlement, my entrance into the world of savings finally had begun. I read about stocks, bonds, and different types of insurance. I bombarded my attorney with as many questions as possible on each appointment. My interest level peaked, and I began to feel that I would always be a woman, but no longer would I be an uninformed woman. I would continue my search for understanding, trust, and honesty in a business that tended to frighten women.

"By 1993, my son, Philip, received his master's degree in psychology and asked to join me in the business. This was my dream come true to know that one of my children wanted to share in the daily activities of the day care center—a business I loved. Besides, why should it be that only men can have their sons join them in business? Philip had been involved with the business since he was fifteen years old, and it was a proud moment for both of us when he joined the staff as a certified psychologist. Since my son was interested in joining the business, my desire was for him to have partial ownership. After discussion with the attorney, I chose to keep 60 percent of the stock; Philip received 40 percent that was gifted over a three-year period. My attorney also recommended that a buy-sell arrangement be created to protect the business and each other's family interests in the event one of us died."

Shortly after, the attorney referred Barbara to me in 1993. She recalls, "Now I don't know why I waited so long to discuss my financial affairs with anyone. Mary's office was a comfortable place where you could reach for a piece of candy. Antiques and a curio cabinet held a menagerie of personal memorabilia as well as professional honors and awards. It was different and exciting. This was not only a professional setting, but also a place where I found an answer to my search for understanding, trust and honesty in the world of insurance and investments."

Barbara's dreams turned into plans that were quickly brought into focus with goals and objectives. She made investments in lucrative mutual funds, and she actively began building a retirement fund. She continued an education process to learn important details and gained confidence. Barbara admits, "Never did I feel insignificant or unenlightened. The security I had worried about and longed for so desperately all these years suddenly became a reality. I arrived at that place in the least painful way I could have ever hoped or imagined. I became a stronger, better informed and happier individual, due in part to the care of a patient teacher. My peace of mind and life feel safe and secure now."

It has been three years since Barbara began a serious focus on her future planning. Barbara has mastered running the financial aspects of her business. She secured life insurance and disability income insurance protection for herself; she funded the buy-sell arrangement with insurance for her and Philip; she established overhead expense protection for her business, which has grown by 1,000 percent in ten years. Because of Barbara's genuine concern for her employees, she created an employee benefit package to protect twenty-two associates with health insurance, an employee sick-pay arrangement, and a bonus incentive. Barbara continues to zealously and methodically save for retirement, and she is on target toward her goal of $1.5 million for retirement at age sixty-five.

Now, the financial world is fun for her.

Barbara has indeed come a long way since her divorce in 1977 when she had "an overwhelming sensation engulf her," and she realized that she would be raising her sons "alone as well as exerting energy to live as a single woman." Her life alone has been a sensation and overwhelming with what she has accomplished—alone.

Another happy note is that Barbara has found love and has married a great Oklahoma gentleman of the highest order, who shares the same values and an ever blossoming love. She and Bob each have their busy lives and dreams. Occasionally, they must spend time away from each other, but when he comes home . . . there's the spin around the floor, the kick of the heels, a wink of the eye and "Hey Darlin,' Did Ya Miss Me?!"

SUGGESTED READING

Life is a Series of Presentations
>   Success Acceleration
>   Tony Jeary- Mr. Presentation author
>   Tony has mastered presentation to help your people skills at work
>   and at home.
>   ISBN 0-7432-5141-5, Fireside, Simon & Schuster, Inc., 2004

Let's Roll
>   Ordinary people extraordinary courage
>   Lisa Beamer with Ken Abraham
>   Honest heart and soul reading from the widow of Todd Beamer
>   9/11 hero. This book forcefully highlights the fact that trag-
>   edy can strike anyone unexpectedly.
>   ISBN 0-8423-7319-5, Tyndale House, 2002

Millionaire Next Door
>   Thomas J Stanley Ph.D.
>   William D Danko Ph.D.
>   This book taught me how the true wealthy people build wealth.
>   ISBN 1-56352-330-2, Longstreet Press, 1996

Pitch like a Girl
>   How a woman can be herself and still succeed
>   Ronna Lichtenberg author
>   Every man and woman needs to read this book and find out if you
>   are pink or blue and discover your natural pitching style.
>   ISBN 1-59486-009-2, Rodale, 2004